presence
is power

presence
is power

seven steps
for living a
life of prosperity

GUDNI GUNNARSSON

 **glow** publishing

Deep gratitude and appreciation for the expertise, support, and aid provided by
Jónheiður Ísleifsdóttir, Ármann Kojic, Guðlaug Pétursdóttir, Jón Ármann Steinsson,
Martin Regal, and Carol Killman Rosenberg

Published by glow publishing
www.presenceispower.com

Distributed by Greenleaf Book Group

For ordering information or special discounts for bulk puchases, please contact
Greenleaf Book Group at PO Box 91869, Austin, TX 78709, 512.891.6100.

Translation: Martin Regal & Gudni Gunnarsson
Editor: Carol Killman Rosenberg
Icelandic editor: Davíð A. Stefánsson
Cover Design: Armann Kojic
Graphic Designer: Ármann Kojic
Cover Photographer: Bragi Þór Jósefsson
Icelandic layout: Eyjólfur Jónsson - English layout: Gary Rosenberg
Glow Publication – REYKJAVÍK – 2014
GLOWPUBLISHING.COM

Cataloging-in-Publication data

ISBN: 978-0-9906227-0-3

Part of the Tree Neutral® program, which offsets the number of trees consumed in
the production and printing of this book by taking proactive steps, such as planting
trees in direct proportion to the number of trees used: www.treeneutral.com

Printed in the United States of America on acid-free paper

15 16 17 18 19   10 9 8 7 6 5 4 3 2 1

First Edition

Dedication

To my mother, Emilía Ásgeirsdóttir,
and my father, Gunnar Guðnason

I am my mother and my father—they live in me,
and this is their book. As I was growing up, they allowed
me ample space for volatility and suffering, either within
myself or in my relationship with others. They shared
with me all they had as well as all they did not have,
and for that I am still in a state of awe, infused
with a deep reverence and eternally grateful.

Gudni Gunnarsson is a life coach and yoga instructor and the creator of GlóMotion. In the 1980s, he began his thirty-five-year career as a fitness trainer in Iceland and became a pioneer in the fitness industry. As founder of Iceland's first professional gym and *Fitness & Nutrition* magazine, Gunnarsson quickly established himself as a leading contributor to the holistic approach to mind and body development.

In the early 1990s, Gunnarsson worked as a life management consultant for celebrities and business executives in Los Angeles. While in Los Angeles, he developed Rope Yoga Fitness, which he later combined with his life coach philosophy to create GlóMotion—a mindful fitness and nutritional program empowering people to be the change in their own lives.

Gunnarsson currently owns and operates the Rope Yoga Center in Reykjavik, Iceland. He is the bestselling author of *Presence Is Power (Máttur viljans,* Iceland, 2011) and *Awareness Prosperity (Máttur athyglinnar*, Iceland, 2012), which are now available in English under the above titles.

Contents

Introduction

"Nowhere Man, please listen . . . the world is at your command!"
—Lennon–McCartney, From the Beatles' album *Rubber Soul*

At any time, we may awaken, take responsibility, and change our destiny. We are immensely powerful beings who have strayed from the path of light and love to experience this realm of duality and fragmentation for the purpose of self-realization and reunion. The separation and fear we feel are illusions, but we have become so accustomed to the darkness and the struggle to feel complete that we have become "addicted" to these conditions. Although the fear is constraining and limiting, it feels natural and normal. That's why letting go of these constraints and limitations and embracing change can feel like an overwhelming challenge. Nevertheless, we know in our hearts that love is the path and prosperity is our birthright.

The opportunity presented in this book is to live from the integrity of the heart where gratitude is abundant. *Presence Is Power* is a concise guide for moving away from "scarcity consciousness" (the false perception of absence or lack) and into a life where we are fully alive and responsible for our creation. This seven-step progression leads away from fear-based thinking toward the purpose of living in prosperity and gratitude. This book contains the answer to the single most important question in your life: *Why am I not living life to the fullest, in true prosperity, with an abundance of self-love and gratitude for my life?*

We each know in our hearts that it is vital to love and forgive ourselves for our perceived faults, but our society has convinced us that there is something missing and that we are not worthy of these things because we are incomplete. We aim to be happy or fulfilled *someday*, but we are so trapped in an illusionary process of addiction to the "norm" that we never do more than react to circumstances. We do not understand that to have the power of presence is to consciously create a life of prosperity. Instead, we remain unaware, often unconsciously choosing to live in (and continually repeat) the so-called past. This repetitive, reactionary behavior is controlled by our emotions, which trigger the biological responses to which our bodies have become accustomed, thereby allowing these dependencies to run our lives.

Addiction is not uncommon among us. Thirty years of study and teaching have shown me that we are all highly addicted to many forms of absence. Although a great deal of attention has been placed on mood-altering substances such as drugs and alcohol, these are only a means to an end—to be emotionally numb. We systematically avoid being present and responsible for living consciously because we have become convinced that our thoughts are who we are and to release them is to lose our identity. These thoughts have been molded by a society that thrives on illusion, and we have been unwittingly participating in society's game of scarcity. It causes us to feel unworthy of anything more. The opportunity here is to change our perspective by becoming aware of this illusion—to become present and reclaim our power to live and create intentionally. Failing to seize this opportunity is to abandon ourselves again and again through addiction and the accompanying distraction, remaining absent to a prosperous life filled with gratitude.

A person who "abandons the self" many hundred times a day cannot enjoy the subtle happiness in everyday life. He or she does not experience well-being or self-love. Instead, this person becomes trapped in a cycle of negative thoughts, fed by negative nourishment and behaviors, which in turn creates a launching pad for greater self-destruction. The average person expends about 85 percent of all his or her energy in resistance or self-pity. Some manage to live to a noble age while finding life tedious and exhausting right up to the end. Others nurture various diseases along the path of life that sap and deplete their energy. Others dispense so much energy from their bodies that they can no longer tolerate themselves and give up and die. But my purpose here is not to talk about death or what leads to death, but rather to ask you: Is there life in *your* life? Are you allowing your life to be run by addictions and reactionary behaviors? Are you draining your life's flame by investing in negative attachments and continuing to live in scarcity and fear? It's a choice you make.

This book gives you the capacity and the tools to free yourself from being spellbound—not the kind of spellbinding we find in fairy tales or accounts of magic. This is a book about overcoming the most powerful spell anyone can cast—the one that entraps the self and causes us to direct negativity *at* ourselves and *through* ourselves at the world. This book is about assuming self-control and taking back one's power. Simply put: all that you devote your energy to grows and expands. When you are present, you can direct your energy toward a life of prosperity and gratitude.

I have seen considerable success with my clients who have been faced with various diseases or challenges stemming from a depletion of energy. These issues always reflect "energetic bankruptcy" in one form or another. When I share with my clients the simple truth that there is no need to feel guilty because there is no wrong or right (only cause and effect) and that they have not wasted or destroyed their energy (only invested or allocated it unconsciously), they experience the desire to begin investing their energy in creating and attracting joy and prosperity into their lives. This is an awakening to one's power and that is the opportunity I am presenting here for your consideration.

The time to awaken to your power is now. You are a divine creator—whatever you believe is what you become. By acknowledging that your essence is pure energy, light, and love, you reveal the miracle that is you! Take this journey as described throughout this book to live life as you were meant to—in prosperity and gratitude. During this journey, you may discover that I have used certain words and phrases in a way with which you are unfamiliar. Please turn to the glossary whenever you need clarification, or better yet, review the glossary before you turn to the first chapter. There are seven steps on this journey—not easy steps but *essential* ones if you are to arrive at your destination. Step 1 is awakening to your behavior. Awareness is the key to transformation and prosperity. It is your essence, primary asset, and the glow radiated by your soul.

Step 2 is becoming responsible for this behavior and then forgiving yourself. Responsibility is the product of forgiveness. It is the prerequisite of sustained presence, ability, might, and will. It is complete empowerment. You then progress to Step 3 where you define your purpose, vision, and goals to create a framework for sustaining and strengthening a conscious permission-based lifestyle.

Step 4 is about commitment. If you do not trust yourself and feel worthy of, and committed to, change, you limit your ability to receive love and prosperity. Commitment is the holy grail of trustworthiness and prosperity. The moment you commit yourself, the universe takes you seriously and your permission to flourish is maximized. Step 5 reminds you that you reveal your intentions through action. You communicate your worthiness with the language of integrity. Advancement is expressed and projected by the frequency of the heart. Every thought, emotion, gesture, and action is the sacred dialogue of abundance. To will is to act.

Step 6 is about witnessing your progress with love and making the necessary adjustments to your mission to sustain a journey of prosperity. Insight is the permanent state of awareness. It is the compassionate witness experiencing the present moment from the premise of the heart. There is intimacy, unity, and love in every breath. Step 7 is gratitude, a state of bliss, and energetic generosity. Gratitude is enlightenment. It is the glow of generosity expressed by blessing each moment. It is the realization that awareness is the primary asset and that when you love fully, you are complete and prosperous: enlightened.

* * *

I trust your mind is open to what I have to say here because I know that your heart is open. The heart is *always* open—all it requires is sufficient room to beat and feel it is being heeded. This book is for the heart that wants to beat with more energy and passion—the heart that remembers its main purpose is to radiate light, love abundantly, and generously share the love so that you can experience and live in a constant state of prosperity.

The simple version of my biography is as follows: I was weak and now I am strong. I was a victim and now I am the creator of my own life. I take full responsibility for my life, whatever happens. For decades I have been engaged with existential questions and have learned many hard lessons in the process. In addition, I have dedicated my life to energy management— helping others through various methods to realize a maximum level in the quality of their lives and an improved sense of well-being. I have learned a number of things from this experience:

Everything is energy and motion.

The only thing we do in life is *will* or *unwill*. In other words, we can live our life intentionally or unintentionally, as a deliberate creator or an unconscious victim of energetic collisions, or "accidents." But whichever we choose, the responsibility is always ours. Remember throughout this book and your life: ***The will is always yours. The choice is always yours.***

Life's greatest paradox is that we do not want what we have, in spite of all we have acquired and desired. We do not wish to be where we are, even though this is the place to which we came. We have unconsciously created our own lack by investing our energy in it through our fear-based thoughts. The energy we invest does not discriminate. In other words, by thinking about what we don't want, we are actually creating it and there-fore wanting what we think and say we don't want. This is what needs to change. This book can show you how.

My Story of Renewal

When I was a teenager I had a very limited foothold. No one had taught me any discipline. I brought myself up while my parents remained at a great distance lost in their distractions. I had become terrified of the passion inside me. I did not know where this passion came from and even less how to deal with it. Everything I did was done with a great intensity, which was because I did not like myself very much. I felt bad in my own company. I was frightened. I literally feared my own power and intensity. I feared myself.

I did not want to continue to live that way. This led me to discover my own methods of healing. I began with physical training and later added meditation and breathing exercises to my regimen. Together, these were the origins of my mindful fitness programs Rope Yoga and GlóMotion—unique workout systems that incorporate the awareness of yoga into a variety of different core-based exercises. Rope Yoga and GlóMotion help to develop one's consciousness and maximize physical qualities through the core. The body is the vehicle and the physical aspects of GlóMotion create an arena for growth and personal sustainable energy.

Once this regimen of physical and spiritual replenishment became a regular part of my life, I managed to reassemble enough of my resources to feel strengthened and renewed as a person. My fear of my own intensity abated.

I had not been whole but divided. With time, I began to bring myself together in order to be an undivided entity. Once I had accomplished this, I have always found my way out of feeling sad or indisposed. I have never permitted myself to stray so far away from my being that I could not find my way home again. This has been a great help to me—the creation of a system of behavior that puts me in direct contact with well-being and a form of passion that is composed rather than scattered; today I now have a framework and a discipline to work by.

I choose to place myself in a process and to honor commitments—whether it be to exercise or meditate, or any other regimen for developing behaviors that support prosperity. I have chosen to keep faith in myself and to honor my word, which is sacred. This allows me to step into the light and embrace prosperity.

This probably sounds familiar, something that anyone can do at any time. But for some reason, few of us actually do it. Why do so few of us want to live in abundance? This is a question that rang in my ears for a very long time. Following a series of financial failures, I came to understand that we are never more prosperous in life than our sense of entitlement to prosperity allows us to be. I saw my pattern. Whenever prosperity was an option, I began to grow frightened of it and pushed it away. I did not trust myself being so close to this energy. I could not thrive in the light because I had only a limited sense of worthiness.

I understood that to increase my well-being, I had to change my sense of worth, and by embarking upon a journey to discover the reasons for my personal belief system and perspectives, I arrived at the conclusion that almost all of the literature and programs available our there proclaimed that *anything* was possible and all we had to do was "get motivated" and "just do it!" I didn't buy it. This is because motivation is always fear- or lack-based, and no matter how powerful the motivation is, it eventually wears off.

I wanted more; I wanted to be balanced, purposeful, and inspired; I wanted to feel worthy and empowered not because I felt "motivated" to change but because the choice to change was mine. Through trial and error I succeeded, and this is how I developed my programs and teachings, which I share with you in this book.

The purpose of this book is to help you increase your allowance for prosperity by providing you with the tools to understand your own power and to show you that you are fully responsible for your existence and the energy that is available for you to command. The purpose is simply to remember the knowledge in your heart and to encourage you to live in harmony with it. It is my heartfelt wish that you discover your own free will and allow yourself to be present to the awesome power of the present moment (the now), and that you understand this notion: **All that you devote your awareness to prospers and thrives.**

By loving and forgiving yourself, you will change the whole world—this very instant. Change happens when you love yourself despite the elusive missing inch or notion of inadequacy, despite what you do in life or what you call errors or blunders, despite any feelings of inferiority that you may have, despite all that negativity, self-criticism, and self-derision that keeps spinning around in your head. When you love yourself anyway, you will learn that there is no bad or good because everything is love; there is nothing but love. When you know this in your heart, you become enlightened and beam like the sun in heaven. Light will shine inside you, from within you, and around you. Your world will change more than you ever believed was possible. The journey begins now with the first step.

awareness   responsibility   purpose   commitment   advancement   insight   gratitude

Awareness

Beginning the Journey Home to Our Self

"I am gold and glory
A loving gilded treasure
I am a gem and jewel
The Lord's equal measure"
—SOLON ISLANDUS

Awareness

is the key to transformation and prosperity. It is your essence, primary asset & the glow radiated by your eternal soul.

Step 1. Awareness

Awareness is not a state of mind but a state of being—an attentiveness that begins in the heart and spreads out from there. We live in a world with thousands of distractions. Without awareness, we cannot choose between what will lead us toward prosperity and what will not. To become aware is the first step on our journey home to our self—all that we require lies within each of us, now. And now. And right now, too. Awareness is active, not passive. It is the opposite of absence, scarcity, and lack. Awareness is our primary asset: how we devote or invest our energy determines our quality of life.

The first step on the road to prosperity resides in mindfulness—in being aware of our current position so that we can genuinely assess whether we want to continue along the path we are on or branch out in new directions. As soon as we make that decision, we are on our way. Step 1 begins when you know this truth intimately in your heart:

> **All that you devote your awareness to grows and thrives.**

This is why the grass is always greener on the other side of the fence. You gaze at it, think about it, water it, and bathe it in the strong sunlight of desire; you invent complex and involved dreams about it day and night, and the grass gets greener and greener. The grass on the other side is in perfect condition, and from where you stand on the dry dirt in the poorly lit present moment where gray everyday routine resides, the green grass entrances you more than anything else in existence. One of the most signifi-cant advantages of the greener grass is that it is not *here*—but somewhere else. It is not *now*—it is later. Very few of us want to be present. We want something else because it is the distance that makes the mountains seem majestic and mysterious.

Are You Looking Forward to Being Different?

"Do you want to be different?" This is the first question I ask people who attend my workshops or who come to me for life coaching or energy-management consultation. Everyone says yes. *Everyone. Always. No excep-tions.* This led me to the simple conclusion that no one is satisfied being as they are now.

If you read this and shake your head in disagreement, then I congratu-late you. If you are content with yourself as you are now, you are a whole being, and I celebrate that with all my heart. However, very few people want to be as they are. Deep down, John wants to be like Frank, but he doesn't know that deep down inside, Frank wants to be like John. John goes around to Frank's place and sees everything through the eyes of scar-city or absence. He sees what he does not possess; he sees what he is not. It is as if he is blind, seeing neither what he holds nor what he is. In his mind, deliberately and systematically, he rejects the way he is, tears himself to pieces, and dreams of being different.

I have met people who have suffered their whole lives because they felt they were too short. They should arrange a meeting with those people who have suffered from believing they are too tall. How have we created this reality? Why are so few women happy with their appearance, especially the parts that attract the most attention in today's society? Why do we always want breasts that are a little firmer or a penis that is a little larger? Why are so many backsides too big (unless, of course, they are too small)? Why do so many people have a traumatic relationship with their genitals, their abs, their biceps, or their breasts?

In a world where nobody feels adequate, we tell ourselves there is always something missing, and we continue onward, forever searching for what we think we lack. And we find nothing except new and greater deficiencies and new dreams with which to taunt ourselves.

There Is Only Light

Remember, all that you devote attention to grows and thrives. Attention is light, and light does not discriminate any more between types of human beings than the sun differentiates between casting rays on beautiful flowers and weeds. Light just is. It modestly shines and radiates to whatever is accessible/available to its energy at any given moment. Light does not shine exclusively to make things grow and thrive. Light shines because it is in its nature to do so, and that is an immutable truth—shining is the purpose of life.

Light is energy.
Light is life.
Light is love.
Light is all that is.

All else is illusion—assumptions, judgments, methods of measuring "good" or "bad," and so on. All illusions. We are absent to the glory of each moment, and yet we think we are free. We are living in an illusionary world we believe to be reality. Nevertheless, it has been claimed that the majority of our existence is dominated by our subconscious, unconscious behaviors. Then, to be conscious, to be aware, is to be free of the illusion.

> "None are more hopelessly enslaved *than* those who falsely *believe* they are *free*."
> —*J. W. Goethe*

Awareness is light, energy, love, and consciousness. Awareness is not our thoughts, and it is not the same as concentration or focus. Awareness is pure consciousness, complete and independent of anything within us or in the world. Here is a concrete analogy to make this concept easier to understand: When you place a new battery in your flashlight it produces a strong and clear beam that you direct at will. The beam is not biased—it simply shines on all things that it is directed toward. Light becomes diffused when you use the same battery power and same bulb but enlarge the aperture of the flashlight, in other words, shedding less light over a larger area. When the batteries begin to fade, the beam becomes fainter.

A flashlight is a simple yet appropriate analogy because our attention obeys exactly the same laws. When we are full of passion and intensity, full of energy and life force, whatever we devote our attention to grows and thrives; it is illuminated. This also applies negatively—so that it affects the weeds in our lives as well as the flowers. Resentment and anger can also be passionate and intense.

So, how is our light diffused? How do we reduce the brightness of our flashlight? By spreading light—internally and externally—over too many areas of our lives. By feeding our souls with fading batteries and poor nourishment. When we are absent to ourselves in the present, our focus—as well as our lives—becomes scattered. When we are captive to memories of a past that no longer exist, preoccupied with a future that may never be, compulsively engage in our thoughts, and preoccupy ourselves with internal and external emotional conflicts, our life force becomes diminished, as does our ability to make things grow. As a result, we become engaged in a vicious cycle of estrangement where the most common solution is to preoccupy our time with material distractions in order to not be present to the lack or scarcity we feel.

Captive in this vicious cycle of dual punishment, we sound a little like this: "I did something that had a bad effect on my life. Then I turned bad to worse by putting myself down as a result. I kick myself while I'm down instead of helping myself back to my feet. Then I punish myself by doing something that is self-detrimental and then punish myself again for having inflicted the punishment." Dual punishment and abandonment equals twofold self-rejection.

Until we have awakened to the fact that we are energy projectors, we are completely unaware that how we devote our energy always has consequences. Energy cannot be destroyed or wasted, only allocated or invested. How we invest our energy, consciously or unconsciously, determines the quality of life of which we feel worthy. We have all that we require—right now—to live in complete harmony and prosperity. All it requires is to stop being absent, choose to be present, enjoy our own company, and dissolve the ego, or what I call the *i-me-mine*.

How do we do this? By attuning ourselves to the frequency of the heart. By reading these words, that is what you are starting to do right now. Living from the heart is a decision you make. Being present and vigilant is a practice that requires breaking away from "scarcity consciousness" and committing to prosperity. This practice takes a lifetime to master, but once you commit to it, you have awakened and have become a conscious creator.

Life is a marvel. We can be responsible whenever we decide to be present, become empowered, and live with intention. We can increase our permission for prosperity whenever we choose by making the conscious choice to open our hearts and loving instead of rejecting ourselves—loving ourselves in spite of everything. We want to be able to say to ourselves constantly: "I love myself anyway."

The Heart Is the Emperor; The Mind Is a Foot Soldier

We are not our thoughts, our assumptions, our perspectives, or our attitudes. All thoughts and ideas are images, bits of information, and how we process this information and what type of images we create are unique to us and always reflect our personal perspectives and assumptions. But where do these images come from? Where did we get them, and to what extent do we live our lives according to them? To what extent do they come from other people? When you watch a movie, you know you are not the ideas or images on the screen, even though it is possible to immerse yourself in them.

The difference between awareness and thought is that thoughts are always attached to an attitude or point of view, based either on past experience or expectations for the future. Thought *always* has attachments and is dependent and conditional; it is a powerful tool, but it always has an agenda. Thought is also autonomous because we only control it to the extent that we are conscious and present. Surely you have had thoughts that you don't recognize as your own. We are downloading thoughts and ideas all day long that do not originate within us but from the *field of life*—the collective energy of which all living things are a part and to which all contribute. They have no power or validity unless we subscribe to or empower them.

The mind weighs, measures, and judges. The heart is much more powerful and its premises much simpler; it just is, and it simply understands. It only wants to shine, to love, to embrace the moment, and to be aware. The heart wants to be attentive only so that we may thrive and grow.

By the way, your heart is beckoning you right now, and it is asking you for your conscious attention. Its only request is for you to listen to its expression. To be conscious and aware is to become present and realize that you are not your thoughts; to be aware is to be an observant witness who loves equally all experiences; not to be a prosecutor, a judge, prison guard, or executioner. True love is awareness, attention, and attentiveness. It requires letting go of doubt and criticism—ceasing to judge or have endless opinions about this, that, and the other.

If you are interested in experiencing the people in your life as they really are, then the time has come to disrobe from the role of judge. Without judgment, all human beings are beautiful—including you—in the very moment when you become present to them and listen with an unbiased ear. They are trusted to be who they are, admired for all they are, and in this environment of care and love, they can reveal themselves fully—as a flower blossoms when it is rooted in fertile conditions, with proper nourishment, sufficient space, a clear purpose, and a glorious sun shining down on it.

To become aware is to begin to awaken and be attentive, not in some random way, moving from one thing to another restlessly, but by beginning to be attentive to that which is worth devoting your attention to, by casting light on the path that leads to prosperity.

Light is always within all of us, even though its strength varies from person to person and from one day to another. Light is always present within us; energy is always at the ready and available—it is simply a question of how you invest your energy and whether the path you choose leads to prosperity or scarcity.

When we consciously invest our energy on that which nourishes our intention and purpose, we radiate light and clarity, love and compassion, and are fully aware and connected to our purpose and passion. The dynamism in this light is at its maximum strength, and our power as creator is fully flowing.

You are a miracle; all that you devote your awareness to grows and thrives. Anything you are not attentive to diminishes. You are a creator—whether you choose to create consciously or unconsciously. It is vital to be aware and to acknowledge that in the realm of energy there is no right or wrong, only the negative or positive consequences resulting from how we chose to invest our energy. Understanding what we gain or what the payoff is from how we are and what we do, whether it's pain or pleasure, is therefore crucial.

Awareness is the first step to awakening and living consciously. Although being present and aware is a lifelong practice, there are some very basic and simple practices you can perform to increase your level of awareness. These practices begin with contemplating some important questions.

Why Don't You Want to Be with Yourself?

Take a seat. Breathe slowly. Do nothing else. How long does it take for you to begin to get restless? One minute? Two minutes? Three? Are you moving about in your seat, looking to escape the discomfort of your own presence? Whether you are an experienced meditator or have practiced other mindfulness exercises or techniques, you know how restless the mind can be and how challenging it is for most of us to sustain presence for any considerable duration.

So tell me, why can't we tolerate our own company? Why are we so boring? Surely, we are just as exciting, attractive, smart, and generous as our friends with whom we enjoy meeting up and socializing. Or is it because when we are idle, sitting still in a chair, we start thinking? Is it because we have subscribed to the notion that we *are* what we think and therefore must be consumed by thoughts when the fact of the matter is that what we think about does not really appeal to us?

Why aren't we in a fully functional, accepting, loving, and prosperous relationship with ourselves? We are often compassionate. We often show sympathy, consideration, love, and support to our friends and acquaintances and sometimes even to strangers. We encourage and support them in challenging circumstances and share their happiness when things go well. We often look at challenging situations and think to ourselves, *Now, I have to be there for my parents, children, or friends. They are entitled to some support from me, to know that I am here for them and ready to do what I can to ease the hardships at hand. That is my priority right now, and I am doing this because I love them and because I am able to do it.* So why won't we do the same for ourselves? Why are we more ruthless with ourselves than we are with anyone else?

Perhaps the amount of time invested in *not* being close to ourselves might actually affect our hearts and spirits (or souls). Is it possible they feel abandoned? We are spirits experiencing a human existence, and in this dimension of duality, our experience of "reality" is reflected by opposites—black or white, hot or cold, up or down, negative or positive. In the realm of unity, there is only love and harmony, no separation or rejection. In the realm of duality, however, the heart feels the constraints of the physical body caused by feelings that are triggered by conscious and unconscious thoughts. The spirit is the light within; it does not feel, nor is it personally attached or affected by our human behavior. However, the spirit or light can be constrained by the human behavior. So, to be "enlightened" means that the spirit's glow, the light, is no longer restricted or constrained by this behavior but is fully expressed and shining. And as a result our relationship with ourselves flourishes.

Everything Originates from Light

Light and love formed the beginning of life in this universe. This is not difficult to prove. Imagine two chambers: one illuminated and the other dark. Imagine a door between the two chambers. When you open the door, light will flood into the dark chamber and make it bright. The darkness does not spread; it submits to the light. Darkness does not flow; it only recedes.

Darkness does not create; it can only conceal. In fact, darkness does not really exist. It is nothing more than the absence of light.

The moment you decide that you deserve the light—the moment you open the door and allow the light to stream in and illuminate your life, then you can be fully alive. You are an enlightened being and always have been. You would be void of life if the light were not within you. This living power holds together the unique concoction of flesh and blood that is your body. You may have often deserted and abandoned yourself, but your journey has always been back to the source, a return to the light, the light that is you and all living things.

You are a spirit. While you are on this earth you have a carnal body. As you breathe, or closer to the truth, *as life breathes into you*, its inspiration motions you onward. The moment you surrender the breath, you expire. Are you diminishing or suppressing your breath, your life force, by not allowing the energy of life to flow freely through you? Are you inspired, interested, and infused with passion for your own life?

All your life has led to this moment where you can reconnect with your source—return to the liberty of free will and boundless light and energy. As soon as you remember and recognize yourself as holy light, a sacred essence of the universe, your light will radiate and touch everyone and everything. You have reunited with the core flame that burns brightly in each and every cell of your body, and with this warmth pervading you, arises the courage to allow the light to shine unconditionally. You are a creator, a generous giver, and a grateful receiver.

You Are a Glowing Manifestation of All That Is Glorious

You are a creator, and life flows through you. You have the power to allow people, objects, and situations to be as they are in this moment because you know that all is attracted and created in its own way. According to the laws of the universe, all that is envisioned or manifested transpires in perfect harmony, and you belong to this precious harmonious whole.

Can you say to your heart that a bird of paradise is a beautiful creature and that its life is special, even sacred? Can you feel a smile breaking on your lips and warmth spread across your chest when you watch a kitten try to walk for the first time? Can you look at a newborn and feel in your heart that this being is a complete and shining manifestation of life itself? Can you admit to yourself that the knowledge of being part of this universal wholeness fills your heart with a gushing feeling of joy and gratitude? We all can. *But do you?* Do you allow yourself to have these feelings and to say these things?

Attempt to say out loud that you are a sacred being, a glowing manifestation of all that is glorious and precious in this world. Was it challenging? Why? I understand your hesitation. I know from my own experience how challenging it can be to bypass the prejudices of the subconscious mind and become at one with the heart, the channel by which we connect to the source of light.

You may have reservations, but if you are still reading this book, you can at least entertain the possibility. Choose to believe that one day you will look at your own life and acknowledge that you are a sacred manifestation, a spirit having a human experience, a holy incarnation. Do you want to believe it?

There is a door in you, just as there is in me. It is there. You know it is. You just have to believe for a fraction of a second, and you will be able to open it. Or at least place your hand on the doorknob. At the very least, shuffle toward it. As soon as you can begin to trust that the door is there, you are on your way. But it requires intention, *your* intention.

Allow yourself to glow. Allow yourself to glow for one complete second. Let go of the opinions, the prejudice, and the doubt for one moment and look in the mirror. Observe the perfect child within. Observe the essence in your eyes—because that is the best place to experience your pure beauty.

In your eyes, you can best see and experience yourself and know all that is and embrace all that you have attracted to yourself. In this moment, you know you are accountable for the light you have created. And you know that it is all good, including what you do not have, what you have rejected or pushed away from you—that is good, too. This knowing, this awareness, is what is required to be responsible for your own existence.

Ask the Right Questions

Questions asked from the heart will change the course of your life when they are answered with integrity. When you ask the right question, you create transformation. Do you really want what you say you want? Is it possible that unconsciously, by constantly thinking about what you don't want and therefore devoting energy to it, you actually want what you say you don't want, will it, and attract it? When I ask people what they want, most are confused and/or reluctant to answer; however, when I ask them what they don't want, they are quick to answer. How is it that we know so well what we *don't* want, yet are reluctant to share what we do want? To will something is to act. Without action, what you say you want has no merit and therefore isn't what you truly want. To whine, hope, or daydream without taking action carries little merit. Until you are willing to clearly state your intentions and commit to them, you simply don't feel worthy of obtaining, having, and enjoying more than you already have.

Some questions remain:

> **What is your purpose?**
> **What is your intention?**
> **What do you desire?**
> **What is your choice?**

These questions are many, but in truth, they are the same. Do you want the life you are living? Do you have what you desire? Why not? Why do you have what you have, and if it doesn't please you, why don't you be rid of it? Who in this world has the power to stop you from having what you want? Ask yourself why you do not make the best of yourself or why you do not appreciate yourself. Why are you holding yourself back? What are you afraid of? Or to put it another way: what purpose is there in rejecting and abandoning your own heart and spirit? An honest answer might sound something like this: "I don't think I am worthy or deserving enough. I don't think I deserve to be happy or to be loved." Be aware that that is your shadow self speaking. The *imemine* uses words like that—not your heart, because the heart only knows love and light.

Are You a Dimmer or a Brightener?

On the ceiling, the lightbulb glows brightly and casts a beautiful light over everything in the room. On the walls are switches—current constrainers used to control how much electricity flows into the bulb. We call them *dimmers*. For some reason we choose to live in the dark or the semi-darkness instead of turning the switch so that we can see ourselves clearly, see the things around us, and see the people we love.

This is the only quantifier. How much light is there in your life? Can you see areas of your life where you have diminished yourself and dimmed your existence? The self-inflicted spell caused by our abandonment of ourselves and absence to the present moment is the real dimmer. It makes us numb and keeps the body and spirit in an obscurity only sufficient enough to sustain minimum life.

Why don't we call the switch a *brightener* or *illuminator* instead of a dimmer? How is it that we know and understand that it takes little effort to turn a switch all the way around until the lights are at their brightest, but nevertheless continue to live in the gloom? We understand this well when we use the analogy of a flashlight and dimmers and also when we sense the power, the intent, and the beauty in a newborn child. But to transfer that understanding over to ourselves is easier said than done. The spell is powerful, and we are numb, unconscious, and habitual because this is what we have come to believe about ourselves. We submit to our compulsive behaviors and the thought patterns of our daily lives like involuntary twitches.

A twitch is an uncontrollable nervous reaction—something that happens without our making a conscious decision as to whether or not it *should* happen. It is an automatic reaction in our built-in defense mechanism. Can you imagine circumstances in your life where you react in a given way without actually making a conscious decision to do so, where you think afterward, *Why did I do that?* Where you shout at yourself after the fact: *Why did I do that again? Why? Why? Why?* An overwhelming sense of anger takes over followed by a sense of powerlessness as the realization hits you that, once again, you have fallen victim to your own predictability and proven yourself to be an uncontrollable twitch.

Compulsive habits are like spells we've cast upon ourselves. We are conscious of some of them and completely oblivious to others. This entrancement has become so deeply part of us to reveal it we have to undergo a metaphorical exorcism. We all know our own shadow, and we are all adept at shadow dancing in the gloom. But that does not mean we do not possess the incantation to lift the spell and stop the dance. We can achieve this by allowing light into our lives. It is as simple as stretching out your hand and turning the brightener on the wall so it lights up your heart, and like magic, the shadows disappear.

How Do You Look and How Are You Seen?

You look the way you look. You reveal your perspectives and your self-image as you express yourself. But who's doing the looking? Who's looking out from the inside? The energy emitting from you is a reflection of your inner attitudes or perspectives; it is the transmitted frequency of your being.

What kind of view are we speaking of? Where are we viewing from? There are two possibilities: from the unity of heart with love and generosity or from the duality of mind clouded with doubt and fear. Are we looking out from the heart when we look good? Our appearance is based on how we feel inside—whether it is love or rejection.

Where does the beauty reside that we witness in other people? "She was radiant." "He positively glowed." "She shined tonight." "He had a glimmer in his eye." We understand these remarks have nothing to do with someone's skin, their noses, lips, arms, or anything physical because deep down we sense all human beings have an inner light that shines, glows, and radiates. We know that the body is solely the surface, and what resides inside is a force as strong as the sun, as sacred as a god. This glory is within our power—when we awaken to awareness and become conscious and responsible.

Do the optimist and the pessimist have a different view of things? Do we fully understand what "optimism" and "pessimism" mean? Does it matter whether your gaze is downward, minimizing and constraining your horizon, or upward, maximizing your outlook?

By changing our perspectives, we change our world; this is the miracle. Our view of the world and everything in it is only a reflection of our own belief systems, and what we see is what we get. When we choose to see beauty and love, love and beauty expand. When we choose to see lack and scarcity, fear and despair prevail. When awakened, we know that what we devote our awareness to expands. We also know that the way we choose to see things only serves to prove ourselves right, whether we argue for our limitations or endorse our glory.

Not only do we see the world differently, but also others see us differently. For example, a few years ago, I ran two workshops on successive weekends. The first was a general workshop called "Fully Alive Coaching," and the following weekend I held a GloMotion instructor's workshop for those who wanted to start teaching my material. During the second weekend, I stood in the lunch-break line and chatted to a woman taking part. In front of us was a man who was in the workshop, and she introduced herself to him.

"Yes, hello," said the man. "Actually, we met last weekend."

The woman thought for a moment and then remembered the man.

"But you look totally different," she said.

"Yes, thank you," said the man. "I just feel so much better after the course last weekend, and now I feel inspired to continue to learn."

We are all aware of this type of radiance. But where does radiance originate? Some say it is brightest in the eyes, and as the saying goes, the eyes are the windows to the soul. Really it is an expression of the whole being. It is the source, or cosmic soul, that is issuing the light. And when the heart has the freedom to beat without hindrance in the ebb and flow of all existence, the soul can fully be expressed.

Using a Rack of Lamb to Experience and Reveal Scarcity

Rack of lamb has been one of my favorite dishes for as long as I can remember. My mother always prepared it with glazed potatoes and all the trimmings every Sunday, and every single time I regarded it as a feast. But for some reason, I have also suffered what I call "lack of lamb" anxiety—an apprehension that there will not be enough to go around. I start to become anxious as soon as it is placed in the oven.

Do you think this will be enough? asks the *imemine,* as it counts the number of people at the table and the size of their servings and then concludes, *I don't think so.*

It is a persistent pattern, even though not a particularly emotionally charged one. I mean I am not exactly trembling with fear over whether there will be enough meat to go around. But the pattern is always the same.

Strange, I cannot remember a time when there had not been enough. So where does my anxiety come from? What is it based on, and why does it keep recurring? Wouldn't most healthy people sit down to dinner and trust there is enough food, especially when there is no real foundation for thinking otherwise. No risk of anyone starving? Is it greed, the *imemine* that brings on the anxiety?

In my case I developed a pattern, a habit that started in early childhood—conceivably a memory based on an illusionary experience founded in the fact that I loved lamb and the Sunday family ritual at the dinner table. Possibly having the ritual invaded created the emotional neurological connections that triggered my feelings of lack and apprehension. I honestly don't know! However, I do know that I am not willing to let these memories catapult me back to my childhood by triggering charged emotions belonging to an eight-year-old and thereby becoming a reactive emotional child as an adult. The most powerful way to diffuse emotional charges from the so-called past is by observing them without reacting to them, and they immediately begin to lose their charge and gradually become passive.

What Is Hunger? What Are We Feeding? How Do We Nourish Ourselves?

Nothing reveals us as powerfully as our relationship with food. We ingest food many times each day and always in accordance with lack or trust. We nourish either our lack or our trust. When we are calm, peaceful, and trusting, we consume enough to sustain our light, but when we are restless and frightened, we feed the *imemine*. One of the most powerful awareness exercises we can undertake is to simply observe our diet.

It is not possible to overeat, only to consume sufficient amounts to feed prosperity or scarcity, depending on which of the two you decide to invest in, consciously or unconsciously. By the same token, it is not possible to be *too* heavy, just as heavy as you have made yourself. Energy can only be invested, not dissipated; on the other hand, *how* you invest it is your privilege. Whether you argue for your limitations or greatness, you must prove your perspective.

Sometimes, we eat out of pure greed, sometimes to hide suffering, but in between we manage to feel something we call hunger. Let's shed a little light on the word "hunger" and how feelings of hunger can provide great emotional insight when we are aware. Let's look at it in connection with everyday habits.

Let's say you've had a good breakfast but come lunchtime, you have to attend a meeting that takes about an hour, and by one-thirty you are feeling *hungry*. Or at least you feel something that you usually call hunger.

It is a special feeling in the belly that everyone is familiar with, a slight nagging feeling, sometimes accompanied by light cramps and a gurgling sound.

Is that hunger? If not, what is it?

The body needs water and cannot be without it for more than a short time, which is hardly surprising, since we are about 55 to 60 percent water. The average human being can only live for about four to five days without water. It's as simple as that. But what about food, how much nutrition does the body need and at what intervals?

Of course, we need sustenance—no doubt about that. And it's healthier for the body if it is nourished at regular intervals. Nevertheless, we can actually be without food for a very long time. Many in the medical profession say it is somewhere between four and six weeks; other estimates vary. The amount of time also differs from person to person and depends on what state of health a person is in. Certain people who have gone on hunger strikes have lasted for over two months. Two months without food!

I am not suggesting you starve yourself. Not at all! We all need nourishment. But it is a necessary preamble to this next question: *What is hunger?* If we can go without food for many days, even weeks, without dying of hunger, what is that discomfort we feel and call *hunger*? Is it hunger or something else? Is this the body calling out for nourishment or food because it is restless? Is the mind looking for a distraction, some way to abandon itself?

Why do we feel as if we need to put something in our mouths immediately? Why do we exaggerate and say that we are "dying" of hunger? Why are we so deprived and empty? Is it possible that we are starving to be united with our heart, yearning to be present and unified, not scattered or fragmented? Is it possible that we use food to reconnect with ourselves, to ground ourselves? Food and our relationship with it is certainly the most powerful tool we have to reflect and reveal how we truly feel about ourselves. Whether we are abusive or loving is clearly reflected by whether we nourish consciously with love or "eat like animals" to sustain absence and scarcity.

Some live with a strong passion for life, others merely trundle along, trying to feel as little as possible. Not everyone taps into equal amounts of energy. But the energy itself is everywhere—in ourselves and in all our surroundings. The fact is everything has its source in what we identify as electricity or energy. All cells are driven by electricity, whether in us or in other creatures. And all cells can either be "turned on" or "turned off"—they can be alive or dormant. Notice how much electricity has crept into the language we use (charged, juiced, electrifying, etc.) If all cells use electricity—do you think it matters whether we eat living or dead food? Is the charge in our cells likely to be related to or affected by the charge in the food we consume?

What happens when a cell does not receive sufficient nourishment? It burns with too small a flame. A cell can be compared to a small wooden stove, and the way it burns is relatively simple. Like the stove, the cell has a particular spatial capacity and uses a particular kind of fuel. To ensure that the fuel burns, we have to make sure there is enough oxygen. We do this by opening the vents. If we close them again we know the flames will extinguish quickly. The formula for burning energy, whether it be in a stove or in an organic process, is as simple as that: *Space—oxygen—fuel (spark of life and light combustion oxidation)*

Little oxygen—little fire.

A great deal of oxygen—the fuel burns too quickly.

Little fuel makes for a small fire—too much space.

A lot of fuel suffocates the fire—too little space.

If the stove needs cleaning, the fire will not burn brightly.

Damp or rotten wood makes for slow burning.

Eating Habits of a Modern Man

We all know the food we eat affects the cells in our bodies, but what are the main eating habits and patterns of modern man? Foremost, he eats processed and packaged foods (which often contain a long list of questionable ingredients one can hardly pronounce). This makes the flame burn poorly because the fuel itself is worn out and saturated with sweeteners, preservatives, food coloring, bulking agents, emulsifiers, flavor enhancers, humectants, stabilizers, and thickeners. Packaged food is handled in such a way that it becomes far removed from its original state, either by stewing, freezing, or various other industrial processing methods that seek in one way or another to extend the sell-by and consume-by dates. It is precisely the process of increasing the shelf life of foods and storage capacity that causes it to lose the enzymes and the faculties to create quality nutrients. The electricity is lost, the food no longer has any light, and it does not give out any energy, even though it may fill one's stomach. It is also interesting to note that the more food is processed before we eat it, the harder it is to digest, while fresh fruits and vegetables are easily and more readily ingested.

Second, modern man eats fast food in such large quantities that the stove fills up and the fire is suffocated. He must eat more fast food—and quickly because that is the definition of *fast* food. As a result, there is very little chewing taking place and the food therefore passes too quickly through the first and vital opportunity for the body to digest it. Chewing is the way we bathe our food in enzymes contained in our saliva. The act of chewing also sends the message to the stomach: *food is on the way!* and stimulates the production of hydrochloric acid needed for healthy digestion.

The process of digestion does require energy, which is why it is also so important to chew and give the body all the help you can. Our digestive systems are designed for us to eat slowly and calmly. Our teeth are there to break down what we eat and our saliva to release the digestive enzymes that turn living foods into nourishment. It is probably for this reason that the stomach takes twenty minutes to let the brain know that it is full. That's right: twenty minutes.

So, let's say we are sitting down at a table laden with food and that we eat systematically and rather quickly for forty minutes. Afterward we are completely full, literally packed solid with food, and as the feeling of a stomachache starts to appear we rub our bellies and say, "I'm stuffed." Why? Because half the time we are eating beyond our body's actual demands, and in doing so, we are ignoring the body's natural requirements. When we overeat like this, we are only feeding the *imemine*. At the same time, we are abusing our bodies so that we can confirm our own powerlessness and create fragmentation.

And what is taking place inside us? The body experiences discomfort. It is so sated with food and energy that it cannot process them efficiently. The stomach needs to use a good deal of physical energy to process the food it takes in. While all that energy is centered in the stomach so that it can do its job, there is very little left to transport the nutrients to the rest of the body. It's a little paradoxical, to say the least, and a rather senseless investment of precious energy.

This is how we use food to dampen the fire in our cells—in our inner-most depths. It is easy enough to pounce on tobacco, alcohol, or narcotics as the culprits to blame for our bad behavior. But we eat every day of our lives and each time we eat, we have an opportunity to honor our bodies by offering them wholesome, energy-rich, and succulent food in modest portions at intervals that support our digestive abilities. But we don't. Or very few of us do.

So many people are constantly engaged in an emotional battle with their own bodies and nourishment and can fill their whole lives with being virtually obsessed with those "extra pounds" and the "best ways" to work them off. This is one kind of vicious cycle based on lack and feeling bad— we feel as if we have been poisoned.

First we feel bad, and the emotion feels like poison in us, but because we don't want to take responsibility for how we feel, we become attached to it. Thus, we must find ways to continuously feed ourselves and nurture this bad feeling, and then the brilliant idea comes to us. *Why not use food as a means to reinforce this bad feeling?* It is totally genius, because we have to eat. It is a vital function of our body. Not only that, but it is a great place to hide self-abandonment and self-rejection because weight loss is such a prevalent and acceptable issue in our culture.

We know deep in our hearts this is not good. This way of behaving is not a step in the direction of prosperity and only makes us feel worse. The *imemine* pushes this knowledge deep below the surface so that we can continue to live in lack; it silences the heart in order to maintain its own, limited existence, thriving in absence.

Absence Is the Only Addiction— Awareness Is the Antidote

All addiction is about scarcity. This lack has many faces. We send ourselves coded, homespun messages about what is missing from our lives or ourselves, and when we take a good look at the matter, it is apparent that society has endorsed a large number of ways to sustain addiction. But deficiency is an illusion. The only thing lacking is your own presence. Nothing else. Always. When something is missing—it is you. You are what is missing—your presence in the now with yourself; your presence without resistance and without judgment.

The physical reaction that we call withdrawal results from having trained our body to shout for something we want and that it is conditioned to receiving. A smoker has certain established patterns in his life—when he smokes the first cigarette of the day, when he smokes the second, under what circumstances, and so on. He thus conditions his body to consume a certain amount of nicotine each day, and he connects this to specific social situations. Naturally, the body reacts quickly when the smoker does not keep to his habit, and like a child who did not get what he wants, the *imemine* throws a self-indulgent temper tantrum.

Exactly the same thing applies to food. We have created a false dependency on food and nourishment, trained our bodies to consume large amounts of food that have only nominal nutritional value, and that is why our stomachs rumble as if our lives depended on filling them. It is as if we *must* have something to eat.

In addition, we have also trained our bodies to fluctuate dramatically at certain signals, as if we were on swings. Food that contains a great deal of sugar, white flour, yeast, and dairy products fill us with low-grade, fast-acting energy—causing a temporary upward swing. But because the body uses up this energy so quickly, it is not long before it experiences a downward spiral, and it is usually quite a fall. The upward swing is in excess of what we actually need, and gravity wins in the end. Whatever goes up that fast falls even faster on the way down . . . and farther than we'd like to go to. When we experience this type of sugar rush, which is only a quick *fix*, it leaves behind an uncomfortable feeling of hunger accompanied by a slight sensation of dizziness.

Of course, no one wants to experience this feeling for long, so we rush off and get ourselves something to appease the discomfort, something to reboot our energy, but that only leads to another sugar rush and another fall . . . and so on. The same is true for every type of addiction.

What has this to do with awareness? In order to change the pattern of daily consumption, we first have to recognize what it looks like. Our presence is required to be conscious toward *what* we are nourishing—a deficiency that leads to scarcity or love that leads to prosperity.

Do you want to radically change your life? It is very simple. Just start by observing your diet. Don't change anything in the beginning. Just observe and take note: you will discover there is no absence greater than that created by the unconscious consumption of food and drink. As you prepare and partake in your meals, ask yourself the following questions:

What am I nurturing? What is my intention with nourishment? Am I nurturing my body or my emotions? Am I nourishing prosperity or scarcity? Am I chewing? Am I thinking about something else—am I absent while I nourish? Am I a leaf on the wind—ingesting whatever is put in front of me—or am I responsible for what I consume and my foresight and planning? Am I attempting to suppress pain and feelings of inferiority? Am I a victim?

Taking a good and loving look at your nourishing patterns is a helpful way to clearly understand and thereby dissipate the illusion of hunger.

"I want to be anywhere but here!"
"I really want a cigarette!"
"I want a hamburger, fries, snack, chocolate!"
"I want *this*. I want *that*."

These are illusions. All addiction is an addiction to absence—a cry to abandon the self and shut out the discomfort brought on by negative compulsive thought patterns that we don't have the energy to outrun or distract from. It would be more honest to say, "I want relief from my mind! I want to be anywhere but here, and I need a fix to sustain my absence by smoking a cigarette, eating a burger, candy, shopping, sex or . . . I want to abandon myself. I am addicted to absence. I'm a distraction junkie."

Anything can be utilized for absence and distraction. Absence is the mother of all disease, and all disease is a constrained heart. The systems we have created and collectively sustain are based in lack and driven by scarcity. Our marketing systems are based on promising solutions to an illusionary deprivation that these same systems create and promote to increase sales and lubricate the wheels of the "when-disease" economy. We collectively create the need and then promise the solution to sustain our absence.

In our hearts we know this; nothing is missing unless we are. Awareness is the key to transformation and responsibility; forgiveness is required to sustain a life of presence and power. On the following pages are a few examples of the most popular activities we use to distract ourselves:

Relationships as absence—*I will be fulfilled/complete when I fall in love and when someone loves me back.*

Religion as absence—*I search for enlightenment and salvation outside of myself.*

Watching TV as absence—*I absorb stimulation and ideas from the TV instead of creating my own and numb my senses in the process.*

Food as absence—*I use food to be distracted by frequently and excessively consuming poor nourishment and by rejecting my body's natural state. Or I eat infrequently and irregularly, and thereby sustain a state of deprivation and malnutrition.*

Alcohol and narcotics as absence—*I sedate my senses and create enough discomfort to last for a couple of days and use that to reject myself further with remorse and shame.*

Tobacco as absence—*I reject my body by poisoning it numerous times a day, fully aware of the consequences.*

Fatigue as absence—*I choose to be tired because it suggests that I have been productive and under pressure; besides it's a great way to attract attention.*

Stress as absence—*I take on as much as I need to create a reason to procrastinate and therefore experience the emotional rush associated with finishing just before the deadline. Or even better yet, I create the circumstances that enable me to not finish and then I can punish myself for being a failure.*

Sex as absence—*I use sex to superficially experience connections with other people because of my inability to love and connect with myself.*

Family as absence—*I devote all my energy and attention to my children or grandchildren and their well-being to avoid having to care for myself.*

Success as absence—*My self-image is completely invested in how successful I am at what I do. On the way up the ladder, I sacrifice devoting time to my well-being, my family, and surroundings; therefore, I can sustain a degree of discomfort and resentment.*

Hobbies as absence—*I devote a great deal of time and energy to my hobbies in order to not be present to the often uncomfortable issues in my life.*

Occupation as absence—*I view myself as indispensable at work and that everything will collapse without me. I choose this illusionary importance to avoid being responsible for life and my deficiency.*

Debt as absence—*I thrive on the shame that accompanies not paying my bills, keeping my word, or procrastinating on commitments.*

Fitness and yoga as absence—*I assume that I will be happy when I have perfected my six-pack, shed twenty pounds, and can stay in the lotus posture for at least thirty minutes.*

The "when disease" is a great indicator of whether an activity is a dependency or a distraction. Even goals can be used to justify being preoccupied in the moment by promising rewards or glory once we obtain the goal or have achieved our objectives. I am not saying that goals are negative; however, there is a huge difference between goals that are founded on purpose and goals that are based on lack and scarcity. A great way to explain the difference is with the phrase *human doing or human being.* Clearly the quality of life is different; prosperity can only be actualized by being present to the glory of each moment.

All Is Energy

I heard a tale as a young man about the medieval scholar and magus, Sæmund the Sage. Apparently, this legendary figure returned from studying at the Sorbonne in France, and as was sometimes the case with scholars in those days, he was considered to possess magical powers. This belief attained considerable credence when the poor estate he acquired on his return began to flourish more than any other in the surrounding area. The envy of the local people was so great that some of them began to spy on Sæmund, and in doing so, they witnessed very strange occurrences.

In the morning, Sæmund would open the barn door and begin to curse and swear with great intensity. As he did so, small protrusions materialized in the hay and then grew into little devilish figures that Sæmund commanded out into the fields to work. In the evening, Sæmund summoned these creatures, and to reverse the process, he fell to his knees, and instead of cursing, he prayed for them with all the holiest and sacred prayers he could muster. They suddenly shrank and scrambled back into the barn to hide in the hay.

As this tale illustrates, all is energy. All else is an illusion. Whether you direct energy by cursing or blessing, whatever you devote that energy to will grow and flourish. The power is in your hands. We can choose to worry and pray for our limitations, or we can begin to devote our light to encourage and grow the blessings all around us. Sæmund reared his imps with curses, but they were also diminished by his blessings and love.

There is no right or wrong in the realm of energy; however, there are always consequences and the company you keep will eventually reveal your true colors. Sæmund's estate may have benefitted temporally from his sorcery, but when you "do a deal with the devil," your soul is at stake. This is not prosperity, although it illustrates that whatever you feed or nurture will thrive, negative or positive, and may end up devouring you at some point.

The same applies to our constant companion—the *imemine*—that we choose to nourish and care for, or absently ignore. Willingly or unwillingly, all that we devote our awareness to grows and thrives. Becoming aware is the beginning of living a life of liberty, free from the tyranny of the *imemine*, free from reacting from our addictions and distractions and willingly creating a life of prosperity from moment to moment by choosing love.

The way to sustain awareness is to be fully and unconditionally responsible for your own existence. Awareness is the key to transformation and being responsible is the door.

daily reflections

Reflect on the following suggestions. Record your thoughts or experiences in your notebook or journal.

Think about the word "abandonment" and the ways that you abandon yourself each day by rejecting who you are in this moment, now.

Listen to your inner dialogue each day. Listen to how you speak to others. Reflect on whether you use the same language for yourself as you do with family, friends, and acquaintances.

Acknowledge your absence. Every time you catch yourself being absent, you become aware and are therefore present.

Nourish yourself with awareness of what you eat and for what purpose. Consciously and intentionally devote time to nourishing your mind, body, and emotions.

Choose and commit to nurturing love and prosperity.

Responsibility

Responding in Our Life Instead of Reacting

"People are always blaming their circumstances for what they are. I don't believe in circumstances. The people who get on in this world are the people who get up and look for the circumstances they want, and, if they can't find them, make them."

—GEORGE BERNARD SHAW

Responsibility

is the product of forgiveness, sustained presence, ability, might & will. It is complete empowerment.

Step 2. Responsibility

In very simple terms, responsibility is the ability to respond; it is a direct result of awareness. Most of the time we are merely *reacting* to stimuli, allowing our various buttons to be pushed. Reaction is a reflex, while responsibility is a fully aware choice to counter one action with another. When we are aware, we are in a position to choose rather than to simply react.

Responsibility is not a burden that we must shoulder; it is a conscious decision to take our fate into our own hands and not be part of an ongoing series of collisions and "accidents." It is accepting our part in the world and understanding that we are the cause of the effects we experience.

To take responsibility means embracing everything that *is,* without taking a position, having opinions, or holding judgment. It is to understand that where there is love, no one stands accused. To be responsible means to forgive yourself unconditionally and love yourself with your whole heart. When you are responsible, you can state unequivocally: "I am responsible for who I am and where I am, how I feel, where I came from, what I have in life and what I do not have, where I am headed, the basis for my existence, and how well I employ my attention or my energy."

Some may think that it is too difficult to live with such a great a level of responsibility. But this is only true if you shoulder the responsibility with a sense of guilt. Being responsible has nothing to do with guilt, although these two words are often integrally bonded. When I ask someone, "Are you ready to be responsible for this?" they usually take to creative listening and interpret this question to mean: "This is your fault, and you have to admit it! Shame on you!"

I assure you that to be responsible does not mean you have to hang your head and have the world judge you. I am not suggesting that you be responsible for your existence so that you can find some new reason to blame yourself. The word *responsibility* does not imply guilt. Guilt implies the notion of judgment—good or bad, who did what to whom, and what the punishment should be. Judgment is a position, a perspective. Such positions mean resistance, fear, and the opposite of love. Again, to be responsible means to forgive yourself unconditionally and love yourself with your whole heart.

As soon as you understand and acknowledge that being responsible is life's greatest opportunity to reclaim your power, then you can open your heart to the light. In this way, you recover the energy you had been allocating to victimhood and self-pity.

Our Will Be Done!

Everything is done willingly. The only difference is whether it is willed consciously or unconsciously. When we consciously choose our form of daily nourishment, we alone determine how we feel. When we make an unconscious choice, the choice itself determines how we feel. It is impossible not to choose. Choosing *not* to choose is a decision made in favor of lack and powerlessness. Not making a conscious choice is electing not to be responsible; it is rejecting being a conscious creator and instead electing to be a victim.

Our will is always done, no matter how weak it is or on what frequency we are broadcasting. If we allow ourselves to be herded through life, then we are driven by the "hidden agenda" that resides in all of us. The old programming we learned in our childhood automatically takes over, and it is so often built on doubtful conditions and assumptions. The programming is housed in an amazing machine we call the brain. There is also an *imemine* living there, and the last thing this shadow-based entity wants us to do is listen to our heart and what it has to contribute. The *imemine* is the beast of scarcity that sustains the illusions, maintains our hidden agendas, and manages our permission to be prosperous. Until we take responsibility, the *imemine* rules the roost.

Either you are aware and responsible and therefore choose consciously, realizing the consequences of your choices, or you are absent and unconscious as you impulsively and reactively move through life unwilling to be responsible for the consequences of your actions. There is only one law: cause and effect. You invest the energy, and you experience the results. Whether you focus on what you do want or on what you don't want, you are willing it by investing your energy in it.

This law applies to all categories of nourishment: the food we eat at the table, the fluids we drink, the air we breathe, the stories we read, the messages we hear from family and friends, and the words spoken by our inner voice. And especially the latter because these messages echo so loudly, clearly, and for such a long time to each and every cell of our body.

The same laws apply to all these types of nourishment—when we choose positive constructive nourishment we steer our own feelings. But when we make no attempt to consciously and responsibly choose our nourishment, we allow negative or positive emotions to determine our choices and that affects our feelings and our behavior toward other people and the world at large, not to mention the impact our consumption patterns have on the economies of scarcity (processed and decimated foods) or prosperity (organic and living, self-sustaining agriculture).

There are two options to nourish:

1. Our feelings of lack steer our nourishment toward scarcity—in other words, how we feel determines and strengthens the vicious cycle of disempowerment.
2. We can choose greater prosperity and make ourselves stronger by nourishing consciously with intent.

You Are Responsible for Creating Your Life

I always know what you want! You know it too. You have created what you are, all that you possess, and all that has happened in your life. You reveal yourself every living second in your physical posture, the way you dress, the words you use, your diet, lifestyle, friends, enemies, household, children, family, work, and so on and so forth.

If you won't be responsible for having exercised your will, then you are a victim! "If" and "could have" are the love poems of the victim, and most of us compose such lyrics every single day. It would be possible to say here, "*Unfortunately*, you bear full responsibility for everything in your life!" But I am not saying that. I am saying, "It is a blessing, and it indeed fortunate that everything in your life is your responsibility with all its wonderful twists and turns. It is not a curse but a blessing because *you have the power to change*, to turn your back on scarcity, and take deliberate steps toward prosperity.

Only you. No one else. No other person has the power to change your life or give you peace, blessings, and happiness. No circumstance can do it either—not a new job, a new car, a new baby, a new partner, a new guitar, a new iPhone, a new house, a longer vacation, or increased leisure. Everything in this world is bound by time because even though you can experience a short rush when you move into a new house, it will soon wear off. The *imemine* is always there, prowling about, looking for some new wound or regret to hook on to; it seeks any way to suppress and numb feelings of discomfort. This is when the when-disease starts up again: "When I get a raise, then everything will be better . . . "

Remember, only you have the power to change your life. To make the good news even better, I can tell you that this is not a difficult task. Instead of changing the whole world, all you have to do is change your perspectives and your opinion of yourself. The miracle takes place in you, and the moment it does your world changes. It's as easy as that.

But be on the lookout! Society does not necessarily agree with this truth. Most people are riddled with self-pity, accusations, and the idea that it is all someone else's fault. Most of us have been brought up with the belief that we do not bear any responsibility for what we experience in life, that all is the result of an accident. And many of us bring up our own children in the same way—automatic rearing based on accidental decisions and misinformation that comes from somewhere and that we have adopted without criticism by force of habit.

We point away from ourselves and at the world around us, society, our families, the economic situation, the weather, prices, work, colleagues, the boss, bad luck. It is very easy to generalize and make society the villain.

Children are taught that it is boring to go to school, that it is one of those things that we have to shut up about and suffer through, and we ourselves come home from an ordinary day at work and curl up on the sofa, worn out and irritable.

Why Are You So Tired?

What makes us so tired? Who tires us out so much? There is no natural law that says we have to come home tired from work or from school—two people can do exactly the same job and one of them goes home exhausted and the other full of energy. Why?

"Why are you so tired?"

I always pose this question in my workshops and at the first meeting with a potential client. And they are not slow to answer: *work, the kids, husband, wife, social life, financial worries, the car, the apartment, dental costs, the government, my back, indigestion, the next-door neighbor, lack of sleep* . . . and so on. It does not occur to anyone that they are personally responsible for being tired.

"Are you tired simply because you are tiring?" I ask in response. This question does not go over well. Everyone typically goes into denial, resisting the idea that they are tiring themselves out with their lifestyle, unnecessary worries, hypercriticality, and rejection of their own emotions and personality.

Let's look at a practical example. Let's say that you *devote* an ordinary week doing all the things you normally do that usually cause stress: working long hours; having various confrontations with your coworkers, boss, or customers; disagreeing with your partner; having trouble with the kids; arguing with your bank; attending local meetings; going shopping; getting stuck in traffic jams; watching too much television; and cooking dinners. By Friday, you are worn-out and have no energy left. Yet there's so much you need to do this weekend that you won't have any time to relax.

Does this sound familiar? Let's add one more ingredient: Let's say that for the whole week you have had someone beside you, following you everywhere and making critical comments and occasionally shouting at you. This person points out all of your failings, comments every time you do something wrong, and uses all of this to prove to you how useless you are. He scolds you for going to bed late, for putting your alarm clock on "snooze," and for getting irritable with the children. He goes on about your driving habits, your lack of concentration, your work backlog, your pitiful salary, the garbage you eat for lunch, and the chocolate you have as a snack. He points out how impossible your children are and how your partner is even worse, not to mention your colleagues, the drivers on the road, the tax collector, the political parties, the media, the government, and on and on.

Anyone would get exhausted listening to this for an entire week! Then how about for a whole lifetime? There would be no peace, ever—always moaning, criticizing, doubting, rejecting, and resenting oneself and others. But isn't this exactly what so many people experience? Deep down, we are much more savage with ourselves than we are with anyone else. We never give ourselves a single break, and we kick ourselves when we are down many times each day.

Why are we so tired then? Because we are *so tiring*. It is as simple as that. We consistently bring ourselves down with our thoughts and then launch into life's demanding tasks with an *energy drainer* on our shoulder.

When we live from the unwise ideas of the *imemine* instead of from the blessed song that is in our hearts, this is what we become: energy drainers. I was that way for a very long time, and when I am not careful to be responsible for my own actions, I can fall back into that behavior. It wasn't easy for me to look that truth in the face, but I have learned from that truth. When I understood my power to *choose* something other than scarcity, I became happy, free, and *fully present*, completely supported by myself even when I made "mistakes."

Blame Is a Powerful Disempowerment Tool

Whether you blame someone else or yourself, you are surrendering your power and electing to be a victim. Knowingly or not, you are manipulating the energy to sustain your hidden agendas. The energy-drainer mechanism is worth pondering. When we look at it, we can clearly see how we allow ourselves to be victims of circumstance. It is an attitude best described as "self-pity." Self-pity is one of the most substantial ways known to us to reject energy and renounce personal power. Self-pity is a decision to allocate energy to someone who has not asked for it and without their having any idea that it has been deposited in their energetic account. It's like having a whole group of people, employed in keeping one entertained and occupied in the game of "poor me."

Consider this: "Jane is so difficult; she just sucks all the energy out of me." How does this happen? Is there an invisible cable that is plugged into you? If Jane can "plug herself into you," you must have a socket somewhere on your person. The reason Jane is able to suck energy out of you is because your energy is wide open, inconsistent, and in search of a distraction. You are not being responsible for your own feelings and your own energy. Instead, it is flapping about looking to connect up with someone else, like Jane for example.

A human being who is not present and responsible makes use of resistance and self-pity. That person does not want anyone else to "take her energy away." For example, she perceives that Jane is an energy drainer and thereby completely validates this type of relationship with her. Not accepting responsibility is to resist and struggle against the natural flow of energy by submersing oneself in self-pity and going into victim mode, which is easy to adopt. We relinquish our power for the sole purpose of blaming others for what, where, and who we are because we do not want to be responsible for our own life.

"The world is such a difficult place. Life is so difficult. Jane is such an energy drainer! Call up the wailing tragic chorus for me—I can't do this anymore."

This is the victim's role: judgment and self-pity. Together, they form resistance. But what is resistance? Resistance is opposition and obstinacy. Resistance is anti-flow and anti-love. But along the way, resistance is also a lesson and an opportunity to learn from experience, to understand one's own *imemine,* and decrease the number of times it leads to energy depletion. The fact is, Jane is an energy drainer because we are investing our energy in her. Then, we use her as an excuse for how we do or don't feel.

We blame her for our insufficiencies and insecurity. We only suffer disempowerment, or a loss of energy, when we want someone to be what we want and not what he or she is. The feeling of disappointment is what saps energy. To hope is to beg, and expectations are based on how we think others—or any given circumstances—are supposed to be. This is why we only suffer a loss of energy when our own obstinacy overrides our ability to embrace the present as it is. Persisting and insisting in supposing that our way of thinking is better than anyone else's is arrogance.

Stress is a combination of the need to control and to resist being controlled (defiance). It is resistance against the present moment, the now. It is the reluctance to be responsible and empowered. In this defiance against life, we are so relieved through preoccupation and distraction that we do whatever we can to prolong it, to sustain the suffering for as long as we possibly can, rather than being present to and responsible for how we truly feel.

"Who wants to live forever?" Well, not me. Not in the scarcity characterized by the when-disease, disempowerment, and resistance, and on the *imemine's* terms. I don't choose that. I want prosperity and that is why *I choose to love myself and therefore all that is—as it is.* I choose prosperity and therefore my *imemine* is dormant. My heart governs my journey. I am responsible. The same can be true for you. With awareness, you can take responsibility and thereby make the conscious decisions that create the life you want.

Conscious Creator Versus Unconscious Creator: Which Are You?

Who decided to make you like this and put you here? One, two, three . . . you're it! You are always the creator—either consciously or unconsciously. You are an energy-transforming organism; you take in energy every day, use it, digest it, and emanate it. Energy cannot be destroyed or wasted; it can only be transformed, invested, or devoted. Energy never dissipates to nothing. You are a sacred energy being in constant and multiple communications, and you energetically exchange with other people, objects, situations, and the world.

We are always organizing our energy, investing and manipulating it to our advantage. Sometimes, we choose to devote the energy to make little of ourselves or sometimes to appear to be superior to others. We may have delusions of grandeur or act out of arrogance. We falsely associate arrogance with self-satisfaction or egotism when the truth is, of course, that there is just as much egotism in making little of ourselves as there is in assuming airs.

The *imemine* always sound like this: praise or blame, profit or loss, pleasure or pain, fame or shame. We run away from blame and seek praise. We attempt to avoid shame and chase after fame, advancement, and rec-ognition—none of which provides lasting happiness and prosperity. Free-dom resides in admitting to the fact that we are constantly manipulating, organizing, or distributing our energy in attempts to certify our self-image and our perspectives. Freedom resides in recognizing this fact and thereby ceasing to be a victim of our actions. It is taking responsibility for how we invest our energy.

Are you in sync with the flow of life or an accident waiting to happen? In other words, are you an accidental creator or a conscious creator? A conscious creator has a clear purpose and moves the world with intention and wills life to reflect his or her self-image. An accidental creator moves through life unintentionally, hoping that someday his or her ship will come in, hoping for this or that, believing in luck or some unexplained windfall, not in intention or responsibility.

You can never escape your essence. You attract people or situations into your life that correlate to how you feel energetically, depending on the energy inside you and at what frequency you transmit.

> *I determine how I invest my energy.*

That's how a life lived according to personal responsibility sounds. That is the tune of someone who loves himself or herself enough to want to consciously choose how to live life. Even if you allow someone else to do the decision-making for you, the responsibility still remains yours. In the end, it is your fate to suffer or enjoy consequences. In fact, no one else can truly have power over your energy or your fate. Choice is power. Not making a choice is a choice in itself. Indecisiveness is a source of energy dismissal that causes indigestion and constipation. We have consumed too much and have not been careful enough to digest and rid ourselves of unwanted waste in our experiences.

Accident is the product of thought—you create it by choosing not to choose. Responsibility is the product of the heart—you create it by choosing to choose. When you take full and unlimited responsibility for your entire existence, you are empowered.

However, there is a prevailing idea that "life has its own way of unfolding." We have decided collectively that it is romantic to float through life, like a leaf in the wind: "*Que sera, sera*—whatever will be will be." In other words, your will be done, not mine.

A good many people—though by no means all—find it very unromantic to organize their lives. The word "routine" is so often associated with the feeling of monotony. At the same time, living this life is the greatest task that any of us will undertake. We think it is okay to make travel plans, study plans, financial plans, and all manner of other insignificant plans and goals, but we are not eager to sit down and write out our life's mission, for lack of a better word. Which direction are we spiritually heading in and on what basis—or for what purpose? When we are not willing to document what we want or intend, we clearly do not want what we say we want. *Willing is acting*. When we feel worthy of what we say we want, we take action, assuming full responsibility.

With Power Comes Responsibility

Avoiding the truth is a fear of being empowered—the fear of our own power over our own lives, and the fear of the responsibility and consequences that come with power. It is much easier to do nothing and point at other people when something goes wrong or to retreat into the well-known and socially acceptable cry of self-pity. Those people who say they have a fear of choosing also say they cannot handle the thought of making the wrong choice. They worry that they cannot cope with the consequences of the choices they make. This way of thinking is understandable if you also believe that you only bear responsibility for the choices you personally make. There are always consequences in the realm of energy. We have all heard of the butterfly effect. Although there are many versions of the analogy, the classic version states that a butterfly flapping its wings in China can be felt on the shores of South Florida.

Everything counts; every thought, move, and gesture is a form of energy, and whether the energy is invested consciously or not, there are consequences. Simply put, by thinking about what we don't want, we are actually creating it and therefore wanting it by default. You are always the creator consciously or by default.

To simplify this a bit, imagine that I go out to eat with a group of people for dinner. The menu looks fantastic! I cannot choose between the dishes, so I ask my companions to make suggestions. Someone suggests the fish special, so I order that dish. It doesn't taste good. Someone else ordered the steak. That looks tasty. If I am living according to the conditions of *imemine*, I try to determine whose fault this mess is. The person who chose my dish gets my vote. That person is an idiot. The world is an unfair place. Then, I get down on myself and a prayer of suffering begins to tremble inside me: "You fool, can't you even choose your own food? Why didn't you get the steak?" But wait. What happens if the fish tastes good? Even in that case I cannot be happy about having made a good choice. When I live my life like this, I refuse to be responsible for the difficult consequences of my actions, but I also refuse to take responsibility for my good decisions.

To refuse to have a response and to make your own decisions is like tying yourself to a rowboat and then jumping off a cliff into a raging sea— no hands, no oars, no control. In this type of situation, you can get caught up in all kinds of things . . . things just happen, things like getting married, having children, keeping a bad job, and so on and so forth. When you make conscious choices, you are empowered and your valor is optimized. When you consciously choose, you are responsible for how you devote the energy, then you are recharged and invigorated, not depleted and exhausted.

One Breath at a Time

We bear *all* the responsibility for our own experiences and our own feelings. This is true even in situations where being responsible appears to lie elsewhere or with others. Even here we are responsible for our own responses and opinions. Moreover, we are also responsible for having brought ourselves to wherever we are, consciously or not.

All solutions are dependent on being fully responsible for our own existence, understanding that we are where we are because this is where we headed and where we have put ourselves. We are what we are because we made ourselves that way. There are no accidents, just causes and consequences of decisions and actions. In the realm of energy, the soul is responsible for its experiences and attracts experiences on the same wavelength. In the *reality* of personalities, children are dependents and are subjected to the experiences of the adults they travel with. As children grow, the opportunity offered to each of them is to awaken and become responsible. The definition of *responsible* is to be an adult, unified, whole, and mature, and to be able to bear whole fruit, free of attachments or debris from the so-called past, free from the sins of the forbearers.

The solution lies in responsibility; freedom resides in responsibility. You have arrived at the present moment once you have mastered the ability to sit back in your chair and bear it for more than one minute, when you sit in your chair or on the sofa and not get bored—without getting upset or restless, when you can simply be without needing to do something or be thinking about something else. Awareness is a moment-by-moment process. Even if we meditate daily, being conscious is a decision that we must reaffirm and recommit to. Being present and responsible is a lifelong practice— *one breath at the time.*

You have arrived. And you are the power—mighty and powerful, not in the negative sense, but in the perfectly positive and spiritual sense. You have the power to wield your will and empower yourself, by responsibly choosing how you respond.

"Have I Told You Lately . . . ?"

Taking responsibility for your feelings can be complex, especially when you are used to decades of employing self-pity to blame others for how you feel. Here is a small tale about morning gloom, awareness, attention, humor, and being responsible:

I woke up one day not feeling so good, a little blue and my soul bruised. "Poor me."

As I took a shower and shaved, I started thinking about this feeling of deprivation, and I did what I so often do when there is something challenging going on: I attempted to find a *reason,* that blessed reason we all need to find to better understand why we are suffering. Most times, I would look in the mirror and wryly ask myself, *Dear Gudni, why are you feeling sorry for yourself today?*

But not on this particular morning. That morning I wanted to find a reason and preferably one that was not connected to me. *Life is good,* I thought. *Everything's going well at work, the wife and children are happy, my health is good, and my energy level is good and balanced.* Then I started thinking that Gudlaug, my wife of ten years, had a different mode of expressing herself than I did. I often tell her that I love her, but she shows her love for me in things she does, in her loving attention at home, for me and for the rest of the family.

Probably, that's the reason I feel like I am flagging today, I thought to myself. *Actually, it's been quite some time since she told me she loves me.* And then I began to have a rather complicated conversation with myself. While I am devising how I can get her to understand how unfortunate this is, I realize that I am well on my way to blaming her for my flaws and my own lack of self-love. I laugh at myself and my intention to relinquish my power and make myself a victim.

I know my wife loves me very much, and I am composing a

situation in my head that has no basis in reality. And I suddenly find a solution to this feeling of diminished energy—these blues that I woke up with. I finish getting ready, put my arms around my wife, look directly in her eyes, and say, "Gudlaug, have I told you today how much you love me?"

She looks back and says with a smile that I have not.

"Gudlaug, you love me very much," I say, and smiling she agrees. We both laugh and then I tell her about my anxieties in the bathroom. After that I can, whenever I feel I am missing out on something or feel a growing need for love and attention, put my arms around my wife and say, "Gudlaug, have I told you lately that you love me?"

Re-creating Our Perspective of the Past

Twenty years ago, I went with some good friends to study Kripalu yoga in the United States. The course was memorable for a number of reasons, but especially because it was particularly cold at that time of the year even for some hardened Icelandic men like us. Each morning, we went on an energetic walk to the main gates of the estate and then back again into the meditation room where morning exercises were taking place.

I met two of these friends the other day in the local gym. We were all really pleased to see one another. After exchanging a few words, one of them mentioned that it had been twenty years since the yoga retreat. And then he added, "Do you remember how cold it was?"

"Yes," we said, "we certainly do."

"There's one thing I have been contemplating for a long time," he said. "In the mornings, when we walked to the gates before our morning meditation . . . how come we walked so briskly?"

"If we hadn't walked briskly all those years ago," I replied, "we would not have arrived in this place at this time. We would not be here now." My friends nodded, and I continued, "If we had strolled instead, we would have missed this moment."

This story is a simple way to explain that everything we do matters in connection with what has brought us here—now. All that we do matters as far as what's next is concerned. All that I have done has had an effect on me, on my environment, and on the energy in the world. It has all led me to this moment—in this place where I breathe, live, and feel my own existence; in this place where I am, where I exist.

I have made no mistakes; I have done what I have done. I may have caused challenges, discomfort, and even pain with my actions, but never knowingly and intentionally. These actions were not wrong or right at the time, and I do not recall ever having wanted to consciously cause pain or destruction, although I did. Today, my life is the sum total of these actions and their consequences, and I love myself anyway. I am fully responsible for each breath and every step I take. This moment now is the culmination of my actions, and I lovingly embrace it, me. I am responsible.

Am I grateful for existing? Yes. Why then should I be ungrateful about my past with all its good and bad moments? Twists and turns? Forgive and let go because all has a purpose on the road to this moment. Everything. Why should I make little of who I am here and now? Why should I want to be judgmental about certain things in my past, some of which were positive and others negative? Do I not understand that this means self-rejection now? It means rejecting and therefore abandoning how I am in the now. The only thing I own is the now, my now, right now. The now is a wonderful consequence of all my actions in the so-called past—that strange time that does not exist but which we can, nevertheless, change now with an altered perspective.

But if the past does not exist . . . how come we have a sense of it?

My lifespan is not a fixed entity. My life is simply a story. My story: that version of amalgamated moments of the past that I choose to remember. The interesting thing about this story is that it changes from day to day—when I stand in the sewer and try to justify my existence in scarcity, I can recollect my past with regret and remorse. When I feel well, I am full of gratitude and love and then I am more willing to be responsible for my blessings.

Forgiveness means letting go of regret and remorse. Forgiving yourself means becoming responsible for your life and choosing to love yourself unconditionally. When you forgive yourself, you are actually declaring your love for yourself and shouting from your heart that you are present, responsible, and a complete being—fully actualized in this moment.

Regret, remorse, shame, and guilt are emotions expressed by the *imemine*. When these emotions surface, they indicate that we have not dealt with these unprocessed emotions and forgiven ourselves. Therefore, we have not become responsible for how we feel or why we feel this way. This means that we are still electing to be victims, consciously or not. It means relinquishing our power to serve the hidden agenda of the *imemine*.

I am not saying that we should suppress or disregard what has happened to us. I am saying that we can change our perspective and leverage by being responsible and acknowledging that we may have had more to do with what happened than we have been willing to be responsible for until now. When we awaken and become responsible for the fact that we are creators, conscious or not, we can acknowledge that we may have unconsciously co-created our past experiences for the purpose of becoming who we are in this moment. We are not our thoughts.

We are energy and light, but the energy does not discriminate. Being conscious and deliberate obviously produces different results than being unconscious, not deliberate, or what I call an accidental creator. When we acknowledge that we are the sum total of all past thoughts, emotions, words, deeds, and actions and that our present lives and choices are reproduced by the memories of these experiences, then we begin to understand how forgiveness and love are crucial to change our lives. The practical way to forgive and let go is to be responsible for how we feel and to diffuse the emotional charge associated with those feelings. There are many tools that we can use to relieve the spell we sustain with abandonment, blame, and remorse.

My favorite tool is called *Ho'oponopono* (pronounced ho-o-pono-pono). This is an ancient Hawaiian practice of reconciliation and forgiveness. Whenever I feel defiance or powerlessness triggered by events, thoughts, or emotions, I acknowledge and embrace the opportunity to diffuse or discharge the refuse. I immediately connect with the emotion within me and begin reciting, *I love you. I am sorry. Please forgive. Thank you. Thank you for revealing these emotions and presenting me with the opportunity to be responsible for my energy in this moment by forgiving and loving myself.*

The Messages from Our Ancestors

It is our responsibility to become familiar with our "hidden agenda"—the programming that runs our subconscious. We begin by considering the messages we have received from others. We all inherit the tales of our ancestors—how they broke free of difficult situations and why. We inherit tales of how they went through sorrow and pain, how they ran aground, and how they crash-landed. We inherit stories of how a harsh world has played havoc with our families and how nothing here is free or to be taken for granted.

The stories follow us throughout our lives. They exert a powerful influence like everything else that is inherited from our families and through a shared existence and shared feelings. Whoever takes for granted inherited family tales and values because they grew up with them will use whatever messages they comprise to run their own lives. In those stories are ideas about behavior that will lead either to prosperity or scarcity. Whoever flutters like a leaf in the wind and lives according to the instincts of the *imemine* will accept these values uncensored or evaluated and live by them.

But they have no actual value. The messages carried to us through the stories of our ancestors may have been constructed on terms that we know nothing about—just like the woman who always boiled stew in two pots because that is what her mother did, but her mother did so because she did not have a large enough pot. Just as the woman who cut off the end of the rib roast before roasting because she had seen her mother do it, and her mother had done it because her own mother had done it; but when the grandmother was asked, she reported to have done it because the pan was too small.

In this journey toward prosperity, it is important to examine our programming. Where does your software come from? Who wrote your programs?

Are you the author of your own belief systems or have they been simply downloaded and adjusted to serve the *imemine*?

An opinion without any basis in facts is just an assumption. Values, however, are something to which we consciously subscribe. You do not have your own values until you look at the perspectives you have adopted in your life and make a conscious assessment about which of them is useful to you and make a decision which of them serve your interests and then take responsibility for them.

Core values are fundamental perspectives about life and are well-considered decisions that we use in our daily lives. They can be something small and mundane such as "we should always finish what is on our plates" or something larger and more significant such as "marriage is a sacred union, and it is contrary to my values to get divorced." We all have a long list of axioms or assumptions of this nature, large and small. We use some of them each day and others every now and again. We do not even know how we came to adopt them because they do not appear until certain given situations arise.

If I move my life forward on the basis of assumptions that I have not even thought through, I am still equally responsible for holding them. Those who are ready to be responsible for their own lives sit down, look at their core beliefs, and decide which of them they wish to adopt and turn into values and which they want to dispense with.

Assumptions and borrowed values are behaviors we have learned by accident, noted, and adopted; we think they are correct and appropriate because so many people follow them. We imitate and repeat these behaviors in some compulsory fear of being different. This is how we bring ourselves up and our children.

"Don't play with your food!"

Why not? Shouldn't eating be fun?

"Use your knife and fork, not your fingers!"

Why not just wash our hands and use the natural forks God gave us since it is often easier? In many countries people eat with their hands. There is no law of nature that says one has to use a knife and fork.

Where do all these rules come from? Consider the rules you follow and ask yourself the following questions:

- Did I make them? If not, why am I following them?
- Have I considered whether they are good rules or not?
- Am I following these rules because they sound familiar?
- Have I given myself permission to review these laws and values?
- Have I made a decision about whether I should use them or not?
- May I? Is that conceivably my responsibility?

The Ten Commandments are a good example of clear values. But even they should not be adopted without a critical eye. In my case, my favorite types of values are sincerity, generosity, commitment, attentiveness, and love. The philosopher Plato had a very simple idea about a life filled with prosperity. He held great convictions about the influence of the prime virtues of beauty, love, peace, truth, justice, and equality. He believed these virtues were intimately and integrally connected and that when people organized their lives around them, they would flourish.

Time and again we are reminded how little we invest in deciding our own fate and destiny. In my workshops, a substantial amount of time is devoted to grasping these ideas and becoming able to respond in the moment and not react impulsively from the so-called past. And what is revealed consistently is that people have not organized their own existence and are conditioned by default, fluctuating from one compulsive reaction to another without structure. The point is, if there is no plan or structure—only chaos—chaos and crisis become the plan and the structure by default. In Chapter 3, we will talk more about creating a framework based on your purpose, vision, and goals. You are the creator. Whatever you believe is what you create, and that is what you will become. Take responsibility and plan it.

Children Grow by Example

Many of us have been blessed with children, and so they are often the topic of conversation in my workshops. When we talk about being responsible for who we are and where we are, questions like "Aren't the children innocent? How can they be responsible?" are frequently asked and seem to be of great interest and concern to many. My answer is always the same: I don't believe in an accidental universe. I believe we attract into our lives other souls that are resonating on the same frequency or energy cluster at which we are vibrating—or as my father was so fond of saying, "Birds of the same feather flock together."

There are no innocent children because there is no guilt to begin with. Children are dependents, and just like flowers and plants, they are subjected to the soil and the environment in which they grow. It's not difficult for us to understand that when the conditions are harsh, then growth is more challenging and even stifled. The soil, wind, water, and sun provide the basic conditions for favorable growth, whatever the crop may be. When we raise our children with love and respect and provide them with the conditions required to maximize their growth and maturity, they will bloom and prosper.

We are the soil. If we want a favorable crop, we must first pull the weeds from our own hearts and be the change we want to see in our children. They are much more likely to perform as we do rather than in response to what we tell them to do. The environment is the womb of life. We are each the greatest single factor in any child's environment. When we are love, then love is the environment in which the children grow.

Children need to experience life on their terms, not to enforce ours. However, many parents have a tendency to "train the pain" by their example. I devote quite some time to watching parents with their children just out of curiosity. When a child gets injured in the playground, I've noticed that the most common reaction from a parent is to cause a great hullaballoo and shout, "Oh my God, did you hurt yourself?!"

What message does this behavior send to the child? *You must have hurt yourself. You should be crying. You should be feeling the pain that you are no doubt experiencing.*

Now, I've seen children in lively play accidentally bang their heads against swings and other playground equipment and fall down time and again. They either pick themselves up and go about their playtime or they cry and carry on dramatically. It all depends on whether the parent was watching and what his or her reaction was. Either the parent is horrified and runs over to the now screaming child or acts as if there are no worries. If the latter is the case, the child will pick himself up, dust himself off, and continue to play. I have seen this happen so often that I don't need any corroboration.

This might be called the *elevation of pain*—we create exaggerated feelings in our children who express pain and extreme emotion when there is no occasion to do so.

There is a reverse image of this elevation of pain that is equally common. We could call this the *invalidation of pain*. We know this process best in phrases such as "stop whining" and "big boys don't cry" and the like. The fact is it is very easy to get children to stop crying—for example, by directing their attention elsewhere—especially with very young children (up to three years old), and it usually suffices to say something like "see that flower?" with a tone of wonder or curiosity. With older children, often one only needs to lighten up the situation with a tickle or a little horseplay.

This is all very easy to understand, and I, too, have often fallen into the trap of overreacting. But this pattern of behavior must be considered impractical. Firstly, it encourages a display of exaggerated pain and secondly one needs to find a series of devious distractions to stop them from continuing the display.

Children are often only shown proper attention when they hurt themselves or are sick. This is a *confusing* message that has placated many of them.

What, though, of the idea that children should get an opportunity to experience their own pain, on their own terms and not on those of their parents or anyone else's? How about allowing the child to learn about his own physical reactions and his own heartbeat and let him cry his way through pain for as long as he needs to on his own terms? Why is it so challenging for us to listen to our children cry? Crying is a physical and a psychological reaction. Do we try to prevent our children from sneezing or yawning?

Pain is a reaction that should neither be exaggerated nor invalidated. Whoever does either is living with distorted emotions. And at this point it is wise to remember that we were all children and remain so. This applies to us, too.

Responsibility Is Love; Love Is Forgiveness

The path to living a life of prosperity and gratitude is simple. It lies in forgiveness. Forgiveness is the doorway to a new dimension where the addiction to absence diminishes and eventually disappears. Even so, people are confused as to what forgiveness comprises. After all, it is a complex word, much used, and often without a meaning.

Forgiveness is being fully responsible for having created a particular moment in cooperation with present energy. Forgiveness is very radical. It is not simply content with letting go of particular incidents involving other creators and relinquishing resentment. Forgiveness blesses someone else's role in your own progress and prosperity. You thank that person for his or her cooperation and co-creation in your life. You thank yourself for your investment or contribution. You know that you have forgiven when you have no desire or need to punish or obtain revenge.

Love is unity. Everything else is duality, fragmentation caused by absence, separation, and rejection. In the now, there is only love, peace, and serenity. The moment we acknowledge our absence, we are present; we are love. Everything else is an illusion.

On this basis I could easily and happily say, "I am responsible for my entire life, as it presents itself, and I am responsible for those moments that together make up my life, whether they contain difficult or joyful experiences." Then I can truly see and understand with *love* each and every one of them with all my heart because without them I would not be stepping into the freedom that comes with being responsible for my entire existence.

To forgive requires the acceptance of a few facts: You love all that you were, all that you are, and all that you will be. You love all those you have met and all those who have done things with you, for you, and also what they have done *to* you. When you live in forgiveness, you love passionately what others have "done to you" or in your name, even if they have supposedly caused you disappointment or pain—because the wounds have helped you on your way here through the portal to prosperity. Without "betrayals" and "disappointment" by others and without collisions in the past, you would not have arrived here.

Nothing is bad because all is energy. When everything in the world is energy, then everything has the same right to exist. Some people find this a little difficult to comprehend, especially in the light of all the tragedy that is around us. I have sometimes told the parable of "The Cartridge & Me" to help explain this.

The Cartridge & Me

I am energy, and I go hiking in the mountains. The air is misty. At the same time, another individual is walking around in the same area. He is energy. He is hunting and carries a gun. He places a cartridge in the gun. The cartridge is energy.

The man does not see me and shoots. The bullet rushes through the undergrowth where it and I meet. The bullet, this flying dense little piece of energy, meets me and my energy, and lodges in my thigh.

Who was in the right? And who was in the wrong?

Who was lucky and who was unlucky?

What is luck?

I stand in the mountains in the mist with a hole in my leg. What am I going to plant in my leg? A beautiful flower or a bitter herb?

Perhaps I was "lucky" to get shot in the leg. Perhaps the bullet saved me from stepping off a crag. I do not and cannot know— not in the mist that is life. In an ordinary moment I cannot see the wider context of my whole life and therefore cannot say whether any given incident is good or bad.

There is only one way to live life fully, shining and full of light: by being responsible and with full permission for prosperity. This involves doing nothing that is not good for you. And if you do something that is not good for you, you do it by allowing in the greatest amount of love. You do it without kicking yourself when you are down but with a smile on your lips and in the knowledge that you are swallowing the poison and thereby diminishing its bite and its capacity for harm.

When you refuse to forgive yourself, your hidden agenda is to argue for your own limitations and for your incapacity to create your own life, consciously. Not wanting to forgive yourself is an admission to yourself that you do not deserve to enjoy prosperity and happiness. By shirking in denial, you serve the hidden agenda of the *imemine*. You use interruptions, distractions, or absence to preoccupy yourself, but these do not eliminate pain; they simply suppress and nurture it. And the next time it rises up with even greater intensity, angry at having allowed itself to be suppressed, rejuvenated after its stay in the dark, and consequently you need an even stronger anesthetic to hold it at bay.

The best way to address this is by taking out the garbage daily, by constantly forgiving and loving yourself. When you feel insecure or power-less for whatever reason, seize every opportunity to be responsible for your emotions, acknowledge them, and proclaim, "I love you anyway. I am sorry. Please forgive me. Thank you for exposing the *imemine*."

Chasing the Snake

Two hunters walk along a forest path, trying to out boast each other. Suddenly, they are both aware of a certain discomfort in their feet and it occurs to them that a snake has bitten them both. One of them takes out a pocketknife, cuts the bite wound, sucks out the poison, and spits it out. The other one also takes out a knife—or rather a large machete—and decides to follow the snake and kill it. The one who looked for the snake is dead. The other one is still alive.

We stop following the snake when we love ourselves sufficiently enough to be responsible and not react impulsively to the situation. Chasing the snake that supposedly bit you drives the poison of regret and remorse through your veins to your heart and eventually paralyzes you. Chasing the snake is a diversion from your responsibility to deal with the wound. Chasing the snake is the prerequisite for victimhood. Just as blame is the primary fuel of powerlessness. Accepting responsibility is power and life.

Your Assumptions Only Serve to Expose You!

A man sat on a train reading a newspaper. There were two restless children with him who were getting more and more excited and louder and louder. The man sat opposite and felt he did not have the peace and quiet he needed to read his paper. In the end, he had his fill of all the noise and spat out the following to the children's father: "Have you no sense of propriety? Aren't these your children? They are causing a disturbance to everyone and you do not appear to care at all."

The children's father looked up, full of humility, and replied, "I just don't have the heart to scold them. We have just come from the hospital where I said goodbye to my wife and their mother for the last time. I just can't make life any worse for them right now, and I am very sorry they are bothering you."

When we judge and draw conclusions about things and events, we tell ourselves that we have enough information to do so. We consider that we understand the situation others are in as well as the overall context. But we are only confirming our own assumptions. We neither talk about nor think about nor experience anything other than ourselves. When we draw others into our own illusions as victims, we only do so to justify our own victimized existence. When we need to justify our own existence, we have quite obviously prejudged ourselves. Each judgment is a self-justification—each self-justification is a judgment.

To forgive is to release and liberate yourself from judgment. Only you can liberate yourself from your own restraints—no one else can forgive you, and you cannot forgive anyone else. Why not? Because when you say that you forgive others, you are immediately pronouncing judgment—you are saying that someone else is to blame and that he or she is not good enough.

When you forgive yourself, you free others from being captive to the idea that they are responsible for how you feel, even though that in no way absolves them from what they may have done or not done. In the realm of energy, there are no accidents. Energy is manipulated consciously or not, and this causes collisions we sometimes refer to as synchronicity. The common tendency is to only use the term "synchronicity" when the encounter or collision is positive. However, energy does not discriminate; we attract and manifest according to the universal law of cause and effect. When we have awakened and become responsible, we realize that how we have invested our energy, through what we think and how we feel, always has consequences.

However far out or painful it may seem in the beginning, we have collectively collaborated and orchestrated every moment of our lives. We can only absolve ourselves from blame and thus be responsible for releasing our guilt. When we believe we can absolve another, we are exerting control and manipulation to govern others. The only way to be responsible is to allow others to responsible for themselves. We can only relieve ourselves, literally and emotionally. We cannot relieve others.

Carrying Boxes in Resistance or Love

I once needed to move a large number of boxes of books from one storage space to another. I had to finish moving them all by no later than a certain Monday evening, and of course, I had procrastinated about doing this as long as I could. I had counted on getting some help from my brother, but when it came to it, he was busy and I had to do it on my own.

Monday night. Autumn. Rain. Windy. Dark. And forty heavy boxes of books. One sedan. And I was tired after a long day's work. Here was material for a major attack of self-pity.

Thankfully, I took a deep breath and went at what I had to do without any resistance. Instead of counting the boxes and keeping a record of my progress, I decided to deal with one box at a time. It was a little like being a robot, and this might sound odd, but the truth is that when the body is able to work freely despite ceaseless complaints from the mind, a certain feeling of well-being is the result—a different kind of tiredness, a different kind of satisfaction.

The task was not just bearable—it was actually pleasurable. I enjoyed feeling my own presence in my own body. I had a clear purpose and my attention was all on the work at hand and the inescapable fact that I had to complete it—not in self-pity or scarcity.

Releasing the Handbrake

All the parts of a car engine are designed to propel it forward—each part complements another. The engine makes it possible for a car to do its job—which is to get people from one place to another in relative comfort. The braking system is designed to stop a car's progress or make it slow down. The handbrake, though, serves a different purpose. It is an additional braking system, intended to ensure that the car does not move from a static position—for example, when it is parked on a slope. A handbrake is the resistance for the natural movement of the car—a hindrance. The handbrake is a reserve braking system. Why am I talking about handbrakes?

Have you ever forgotten to release the handbrake before you moved forward? After a short while, it will become clear to you that things are not quite as they should be. You look down and discover that the handbrake is still on and as soon as you release it you feel how the car moves much more easily—you feel how much influence the handbrake has, even though you have never really given it much importance before.

Why do you release the handbrake as soon as you discover that it is on? Because you know that you will move faster when you do, that you will go farther with less difficulty, that it is much more natural to drive with it off, and by doing so you will prevent the car from being damaged. You would have thought it absurd to continue with the handbrake on.

All resistance in our lives is a kind of handbrake. Rejection, criticism, escape to absence through food, drink, work, goals, the gym, the search for fame . . . we think we can win a race with the handbrake on. But it's hard and it's tiring. Of course it is.

Look at the handbrake. Be responsible. Release the handbrake. Forgive yourself and liberate yourself from your own constrictions. Love yourself and go where you want to go, where you should go, in a natural and effortless forward movement.

The Responsibility of the Lamb Chop

During class one day, as my student and I were chatting about this and that, I remarked that I was feeling a little full. I told them how I had arrived home late the previous evening to be welcomed by a wonderful aroma that tickled my taste buds. My wife, Gudlaug, directed me to the oven where inside were four lamb chops, cooked in butter and coated in breadcrumbs, accompanied by a large helping of fried onions just the way my grandmother used to prepare them.

Although I was not exactly hungry, I decided to eat two of the chops. With full awareness, I ate, chewed, ingested, and loved them. When I had finished the two chops, I convinced myself I wanted some more and ate another half. I felt good. I had enjoyed the meat, the onions, and life itself. Then I noticed it was 9:30. An hour later I went to bed.

"What got me so full?" I asked my students.

One student said it was the butter. Another said it was the bread-crumbs. A third guessed the onions. A fourth thought it was likely that my fullness was because I ate so late at night.

I rejected all these explanations. And here's what I told them: "I stuffed myself. *I* am entirely responsible for feeling this way."

You can't eat too much or too little, only enough to suffer, suppress, and limit your metabolism and therefore your energy. Or you can nourish prosperity by sufficiently fueling your furnace and therefore maximizing its energy efficiency and output. When we abuse ourselves with food, the hidden agenda is always to limit the gains possible from our investment in the food we consume, to actually punish ourselves. Nothing reveals our prosperity or lack as blatantly as our relationship with food does.

My students were quiet and contemplative so I asked them if they realized the potential created by bringing awareness to the way we nourish and to what we nourish. They all answered yes. I then asked if they were ready to be responsible for how they felt about food and the consequences of their consumption. The answer was a resounding, yet reluctant, yes!

I then asked why they were so reluctant? They agreed that the relationship they had with food was a serious long-term and unconscious affair that they had not been ready to examine and/ or change until I brought attention to the potential. They agreed to having given a great deal of thought to what they ate but not given any thought to what they were feeding or nourishing. They realized that when they ate unconsciously, they were feeding their hidden agendas not nurturing prosperity and wellness. They were feeding the *imemine* by default.

Releasing the Refuse of the So-called Past

We are energy transformers; we take in nourishment and information, energy from nature or from other people, and then we digest that energy. We utilize the elements that are to our advantage and then eliminate the refuse. Isn't that right?

Feces are not everyone's favorite topic of conservation, but I have a special interest in them for many reasons. I discuss them often—and usually it does not take me more than one workshop to get people to rid themselves of their embarrassment when discussing bowel movements. And that's exactly how things should be.

Feces are one of the best analogies I know for one's emotions, as long as we have accepted that we are energy transformers both physically and psychologically.

"Have you ever chased waste out to sea?" I often ask.

I really like this question. No one ever says yes. Even so, everyone understands that we "digest" life in one sense. When something arises, the soul goes through a particular process, using what it requires and making waste out of what is not deemed useful. The soul prepares itself to be rid of the "waste" that goes with certain situations or events, prepares to be rid of it according to standard methods. The soul prepares itself to eliminate. It wants to discharge, to forgive, separate itself from, release; the soul wants to love; it does not to hang on to something that does not exist here and now. The soul wants to forgive. The soul wants to let go, and release the refuge of the so-called past. It knows its responsibility and that love is all there is.

But the *imemine* does not want to let go at all. The mind wants to be preoccupied, run its programs, its game of duality, the infamous I-me-mine game. The mind spins a strong thread, tying it around any waste. When the soul is ready to flush it down the toilet, there's always that BUT. For instance:

"I've completely come to terms with what happened *BUT. . .*"

"I live in the now, *BUT* that does not change the fact that Dad was an awful parent. . ."

"I've completely forgiven Jonny, *BUT* then he was really nasty to me again and I remembered what he did to me ten years ago."

These days, a great many people are willing to admit the now is the only thing we have, the only thing that really exists. But . . .

At the same time, many people tend to keep a strong piece of string tied around the waste they would have flushed long ago if they could let go of uncomfortable and negative feelings . . . BUT, when all is said and done, the *imemine* grabs the end of the string and pulls the package up to the surface with lightning speed.

Of course, people vary in how much they have invested in the waste of the past. The fact is that many of us never let go of anything that has happened. Instead, we hang on to much of our experience by thousands of strings. And when we are bored and become restless, it is a popular party game to look for the end of the string every now and again just to make sure it is definitely there.

To forgive is the epitome of release for the soul—the best way to lift the spell of remorse and regret and the role of the judge. To forgive oneself is to free oneself from the bonds of illusion. Forgiveness is the most important achievement of your life—nothing else can give you as much freedom as forgiving yourself. To forgive yourself actually means that you love yourself and are willing and able to be love.

In order to free yourself, choose:

To forgive yourself for your own behavior.

To thank whomever is concerned for their contribution to your life—to bless their contribution as an indispensable part of your own progress.

When you thank others for their contribution, you do not need to forgive them. Remember, you cannot forgive anyone else because this places you in the role of judge. By "forgiving" someone, you are saying that the other person's behavior has been harmful or inappropriate. That produces a judgment and comprises a resistance—and that precludes love.

Because there is only one love.

And there is just now.

And it's all in your hands. Your moment is your responsibility.

People who hold on to many strings are not only highly preoccupied (and therefore absent and incomplete), but they also emit a bad odor. Other nearby souls smell this stench. Some people draw closer (those who need to and want to), but most people move in the opposite direction. Another group never makes up their minds one way or the other and therefore cannot be rid of the foul-smelling individual. The choice is always yours.

To forgive is not complicated. To forgive is to be responsible and choose love. To forgive lightens the load. One just lets go. Eliminates. But there is no one who can do it except you.

To simplify the process of forgiveness it may be helpful to consider what your gain is. If you relinquish remorse, regret, and self-pity, what do you gain? Or if you choose to hold on to your stories of victimhood and disempowerment, what then is your gain? Or you can ask the question: What do I have invested in my victim stories?

Being Responsible Is an Act of Love

When I have truly forgiven myself, I have exonerated (within myself) others of the blame and all desire or need to punish them or myself. Thoughts of revenge and the idea of guilt disappear.

Can you imagine the magnitude of energy you could unleash when you stop trying to work out who is to blame for anything? When you stop waiting for other people to say that they are sorry? This is what being responsible for one's own existence entails—deciding to invest your energy in prosperity and not in scarcity. To forgive means to be fully responsible for your life, and to be responsible means forgiving fully, free of the poison, regret, and remorse. To forgive yourself is to love yourself.

Being responsible is an act of love. Being responsible means not judging. It means experiencing things as they are. Being responsible is forgiving yourself and loving yourself all the same—in spite of all the lack that the *imemine* thrives on.

Forgive yourself and choose to be fully responsible. Free yourself from the illusions of the *imemine*—by loving yourself wholly in the here and now!

daily reflections

Reflect on the following suggestions. Record your thoughts
or experiences in your notebook or journal.

Notice when you victimize yourself and surrender your power to
others, blaming them for how you feel. Love yourself anyway.

Be aware of where you are and how you arrived at
this point in your life. Love yourself—now.

Practice being fully responsible for how you feel—right now.

Practice forgiving yourself and relinquishing regret and remorse,
loving yourself.

Think about whether you are choosing prosperity or lack and what
your payoff is.

Consider if you are employing your energy consciously, intentionally,
and responsibly.

Purpose
Living Purposefully and Being Inspired

"Your purpose in life is to find your purpose and give your whole heart and soul to it."

—GAUTAMA BUDDHA

Purpose

is the foundation of prosperity.
It is the inspired light powering
the vision that outlines your goals.
It is the premise of passion & joy.

Step 3. Purpose

Purpose is the foundation of goals. Once we are aware and have made a choice to respond, we will want to express our vision and establish our goals. First, we become aware of being in the present; then we choose the direction we want to go next. Purpose is a route comprised of goals. It is what we want to achieve and our strategy for achieving it.

The language of purpose differs according to each individual, but purpose, as the foundation for prosperity, is always love. Goals based on purpose are experienced and actualized in the present moment. Without this foundation, we slip back into an endless cycle of scarcity and absence.

The purpose of life is to awaken and acknowledge your own free will. Being responsible for your own life is a choice. It is in your hands to choose which path you are on and what strings you wish to hold on to. Proclaiming your purpose—"the why of life"—is the primary foundation of prosperity. Knowing where you are headed helps you determine that which will lead you along the right path. Seneca stated, "When a man does not know what harbor he is making for, no wind is the right wind."

Being purposeful is the essence of prosperity. It serves in life to provide direction and stability, much like a rudder stabilizing a vessel. Purpose is the source of the inspiration; it is what fuels your vision. Vision stipulates the framework for your goals, which are actualized moment by moment.

This step is about harnessing the energy that is recovered when you let go of remorse and regret by forgiving yourself and being responsible for your life. Forgiveness affords you the ability to direct and invest your energy intentionally. Step 3 is about consciously declaring your intentions and being fully aware of the consequences initiated by your actions. It is about asserting your power, free will, and being a deliberate creator.

Purpose is the foundation of being. Goals are the foundation of doing. When your goals are not based on purpose, they are founded on lack. In this case, goals become a pursuit to sustain absence and preoccupation. Although it sounds contradictory, chasing goals as a means to an end is merely an addiction to absence.

Enlightened beings experience the true glory of their goals moment by moment. These beings base their goals on a purpose constructed from values that have been conceived from virtues; however, what allows effortless moment-by-moment success of these goals is an inspired and purposeful vision. When we break this idea down, it looks something like this:

- **Virtues** are intangible phenomena, moral excellence, or righteousness such as beauty, truth, justice, chastity, temperance, charity, diligence, patience, kindness, and humility.
- **Values** are foundational ideas, which are slightly more tangible than virtues, such as prosperity, helpfulness, sincerity, and generosity. Values are the cornerstones of purpose. To understand the difference between *virtue* and *value,* it is helpful to consider the distinction between truth and honesty. *Truth* simply is, while *honesty* needs to be practiced.
- **Vision** is what you allow yourself to see or visualize—images or "mind movies" that reveal your self-image. The visions you project internally and then externally determine your ability to create prosperity and to provide for yourself. Vision is the aspiration—that which encourages your progress. In your vision, you reveal your allowance for increased prosperity because you can never get any further than where you are able to see yourself being. What you see is what you get, consciously or not.
- **Purpose** is the foundation of happiness and is paramount for sustaining prosperity. It is the "why" in why do you do what you do? What are you aiming for in what you do? What role do you want to enact? What is the reason for your life?

The question "What is my purpose?" is possibly the most significant question you can ever ask yourself. Nothing I know of will disclose as much about you in one inquiry. When you are ready to ask the question, you are awakened and aware of your responsibility as a conscious creator and have realized the significance of declaring your intentions.

Purpose Is the Foundation and the "Why" of Goals

Without purpose, goals are only a means to an end, the destination. When goals are based on and inspired by purpose, they are achieved moment by moment. They are no longer a means to an end; they are the reason for being and experiencing love—creation in the now.

The goals are tools, a means to an end. *How* are we going to accomplish our vision? How are you going to work purposefully and realize your vision? By following which routes? In which areas? How are you going to categorize your contribution to the world at large? How do you want to love and employ the light?

Goals are the blueprint for our vision, the framework we use to keep our word and manage our schedule, our intentions. Without goals there are no boundaries and when we have no boundaries, chaos becomes the framework by default. A goal is a written itinerary of destination points along the way that are decided upon with dates and boundaries. Goals are S.M.A.R.T.: Specific, Measurable, Attainable, Relevant, and Timely.

Identifying and Developing S.M.A.R.T. Goals

Let's take a look at each of these qualities—*specific, measurable, attainable, relevant,* and *timely*—in turn. As you read the following discussions, think of a potential goal and the commitment supporting it. Use the process to identify the qualities and resources you already enjoy and also to identify the potential challenges you face. Detect and acknowledge whether the framework or the prospect of structuring your goals feels emotionally constraining or liberating. Use this information to adjust your approach.

Specific

A specific goal maximizes your ability to accomplish your intention. A general goal minimizes your potential outcome. When setting specific goals, answer the six "W" questions:

- What—What do I want?
- Who—Who is involved?
- Where—Identify a location.
- When—Establish a time frame.
- Which—Identify requirements and challenges.
- Why—Identify the purpose for accomplishing the goal.

A general goal might be, "Become fit and lean." But a specific goal might be, "Exercise three days a week, do daily breathing exercises for fifteen minutes, take the stairs instead of the elevator, chew everything I ingest consciously, decrease my food intake by 50 percent, and drink eight glasses of water throughout the day."

Measurable

Establish parameters for measuring progress toward the attainment of each goal you set. When you measure your progress, you reinforce your resolve. To determine if your goal is measurable, ask questions such as how much and how many? How will I know when it is accomplished?

Attainable

The moment you identify goals that are most important to you, you begin to actualize them. You generate permission by identifying what you want and declaring the purpose and the vision that promote the attitudes, abilities, skills, and financial capacity required to obtain them. You begin recognizing opportunities that propel you toward the attainment of your goals at the pace you allow progression.

When you allow yourself to write down your goals you elevate your self-image. You begin to see yourself as worthy of these goals and develop the traits and personality that allow you to achieve and sustain prosperity. Documenting your goals precisely is like planting seeds in fertile soil and then celebrating the crops.

Relevant

Goals must represent an objective toward which you feel worthy and are willing and able to permit yourself to achieve. A goal is relevant only if you truly *believe* you are worthy of achieving it. Only relevant goals support your purpose. Challenging goals are often easier to achieve than less challenging ones because enduring effort requires purpose and inspiration. Some of the most challenging goals you ever accomplished actually feel easy simply because they were inspired by love.

Timely

A goal should be established within a specific time frame. With no borders or time constraints, there's no sense of urgency. For example, if you want to reduce your body weight by ten pounds, when do you want to achieve that weight loss? "Someday" won't work. However, if you anchor it within a time frame and say, "By May 1st," for example, then you've committed your unconscious mind to begin working on the goal and the progress is measurable.

The "T" in S.M.A.R.T. can also stand for *tangible*. A goal is tangible when you can experience it through one of the senses—taste, touch, smell, sight, or hearing. When you can see it, you can feel it. Once you visualize your goals, the projection has begun at the rate of your inspired frequency, and manifestation will occur according to your ability and sense of worthiness to receive your creation.

An Implementation Strategy

An implementation strategy is a more detailed version of your goals—how do you intend to execute your progress, for example, in the light of the expectations you permit yourself to have? What tasks are going to promote your progress toward your goals?

In direct procedures one could envision a plan: You sit down and review your values and decide that *helpfulness* is one of them. With helpfulness as a guiding light, you can decide your purpose: *"I love the world and serve by doing good."*

You use this purpose as the foundation for your goals—and make it S.M.A.R.T.: specific, measurable, attainable, relevant, and timely. For example, you set yourself several goals:

1. To join the Red Cross before January 1, 2016.
2. To travel to Africa before June 1, 2016.
3. Devote a year of service in Africa.

Your vision is in harmony with your goals. Vision is the inspiration, the passion—the source of power/strength/empowerment—yet immeasurable and undated. Vision can change from day to day. How you see the world and how your perspectives can change is influenced or affected by your emotions and energy levels moment by moment. However, when your purpose is clear, your vision is vivid and stable. When you have a clear and ambitious vision that is not undermined by lack, the quality of your goals will reflect your ambitions. You will not progress any farther than you allow yourself to see. When your passion is limited and therefore purpose is lacking and the aspiration to achieve is weak, your vision will be limited. Vision is the inspiration for creating goals. When you cannot envision what you wish to manifest, your purpose is in vain, and the creation of goals becomes futile. Then, you know it's time to reevaluate your purpose.

Your vision reveals your worthiness—how high you allow yourself to soar. Vision is never clearer than the heart allows it to be. If passion is not great enough to illuminate the vision, then purpose will remain obscure. If purpose is obscure, then passion will not be sufficient to keep the vision alive. Ask yourself these questions:

- What do you want? Are you absolutely sure you want what you say you want?
- Have you been acting on behalf of what you want? If not why?

- Why do think you want what you say you want?
- What is your vision and how do you see your life unfolding as you express and project these images?
- What are your goals? How will they manifest? What is your strategy?
- Do you feel worthy of achieving these goals and being prosperous?

The Journey That Was Never Taken

Purpose is the underlying premise that colors all deeds. We prepare ourselves for a journey, get everything ready, and enjoy the preparations. The preparations are formative and influence who we are and how we live. Yet we never know whether the journey will be undertaken.

My teacher Gísli Sighvatsson read me the tale "The Journey That Was Never Taken" by Sigurður Nordal when I was twelve years old. This parable had such a great influence on me that I literally would not be who I am now if I hadn't heard it.

It is about a young Roman nobleman in the second century A.D., named Lucius. The young man had inherited considerable wealth from his father but squandered it in profligacy. The emperor, Marcus Aurelius, decided to take some action in the case and summoned Lucius to a meeting where he informed him that he would be sent on a secret mission to unknown lands at the end of three years, a journey on which he would encounter hardship and danger but where the welfare of the Roman Empire itself would be at stake.

Lucius answered this summons by changing his life. In order to prepare himself, he stopped his debauchery, began to practice sports, ran his household meticulously, and learned as much as he could about foreign and distant lands. After a period of three years, he realized the call might come at any moment and each day became precious to him:

His days became as pearls on a necklace, each new pearl more beautiful and precious than the last because it glowed with the light of time past with greater brightness and he always remembered that the pearl that lay in his palm today might be the last in the necklace. He greeted each day with a strange joy and frequently said to himself: "I love this day because it brings me closer to my journey, which is the goal of my life. Or is it perhaps not a sufficient goal in itself?"

After a whole ten years, the emperor Lucius finally summoned him to court:

You have prepared yourself well and bravely for this journey that your emperor has planned for you. You stand before me now to face any deed or task I assign to you. You have fulfilled your duty. It now remains for me to do mine and release you from this obligation. The journey that I spoke of will never be undertaken.

At the beginning of the tale Marcus Aurelius sent one of his sages, disguised as a singer, to spy on Lucius and his lechery. The sage sang a few songs for Lucius and the guests at his banquet—about the futility of a debauched existence, the advantages of a life of virtue, achievements in battle and human relations, the peace of solitude, and the mediations of philosophy—and from the reactions of the young man, the sage was able to assess his inner values and desires.

He told the emperor about his experience of Lucius and that the young leader was weary of banquets but that he lacked the initiative to stop holding them. The sage advised Marcus that it would be best to "have Lucius conscripted immediately into the army and thus force him to change his ways."

Instead of forcing Lucius to change, Marcus Aurelius created a set of circumstances that sharpened the young man's wits and deepened his understanding and helped him evolve his inner potential. By giving Lucius a purpose, Marcus Aurelius changed his life into a *journey that was undertaken*—with full capacity, awareness, and brimming with enthusiasm.

Purpose changed the course of Lucius's life from debauchery to a life of prosperity. His mission became the rudder in his life, a reason to change his destiny from lack and despair to joy and prosperity.

When I heard this story as a twelve-year-old I was deeply moved, presumably because my life at the time was seriously impacted by the alcoholic behavior of my parents and the lack of boundaries and conscious positive guidance I felt deprived of. The tale deeply impacted me and later became a subconscious rudder, at a time in my life when it was absolutely crucial for me to shape up.

By the time I was fifteen, my emotional ship had run aground. I had started drinking alcohol. I was abusive and out of control. I felt ashamed of myself, my parents, and my life. I was afraid of my own intensity, and I didn't trust myself. I feared myself. I was depressed and covertly wished to enroll in the military to be shipped away to boot camp in order to gain perspective and obtain some discipline, even enforced discipline. I decided that something drastic had to be done. I then remembered the story of the journey and decided to tailor my own life in the manner Marcus had done for Lucius. That's how my journey of prosperity began. The story faded into the background and became a part of my fabric, but to this day I still read the story to remind myself of my blessings and to keep me inspired.

Goals Motivated by Fear Versus Goals Inspired by Purpose

We all know that we can achieve anything we set our mind to. Yet we claim we want life to be a certain way without taking action or we take nominal action and procrastinate, only sustaining our subconscious hidden agendas and argue for our limitations.

I know this make no rational sense; however, our actions communicate with more clarity than words. When we acknowledge the law of cause and effect and that prosperity is *permission based,* we will allow ourselves to put pencil to paper (or seed to soil) and declare our purpose, and write down our goals with the conscious intention of achieving them. Until then, we are likely to use goal setting the same way we use daydreaming: to sustain our absence and not allow ourselves to achieve them, or as some say, "reach" them. Daydreaming and unspecified goals are only tools for creating and sustaining lack. Daydreams without action eventually turn into nightmares.

Another fact worth considering is that most people use goals to chase achievement and/or to flee depravity. In modern-day culture, we refer to the "motivational factors" of goal setting. What I am saying here, however, is that when we base goals on lack or the fear of not being enough, we become infected with the when-disease. Since all we devote our awareness to grows and expands, we only create and get more of what we claim we don't want.

There is an enormous difference between goals motivated by fear and goals inspired by purpose. The primary difference being that fear-based goals happen "supposedly when" you arrive and then you presumably become "good enough." Purposeful goals are actualized in the moment; you enjoy the journey even though you keep the destination in mind. You experience and enjoy the fruit of your labor and love in the now.

It is estimated that less than 5 percent of the population set goals and that 95 percent of them achieve them.

A study conducted by Dave Kohl, professor emeritus at Virginia Tech, revealed that 80 percent of Americans say they don't have goals. Another 16 percent do have goals, but not in writing. Less than 4 percent write down their goals, and less than 1 percent reviews them. This fraction of Americans earns nine times more, over the course of their lifetimes, than those who don't set goals.

In the book *What They Don't Teach You at Harvard Business School,* Mark McCormack sites a study conducted in the 1979 Harvard MBA program. The students were asked, "Have you set clear, written goals for your future and made plans to accomplish them?" Only 3 percent of the graduates had written goals and plans; 13 percent had goals; however, they were not in writing; and 84 percent had no specific goals at all.

Ten years later, the members of the class were interviewed again. The 13 percent of the class who had goals were earning, on average, twice as much as the 84 percent who had no goals at all. And the 3 percent who had clear written goals? They were earning, on average, ten times as much as the other 97 percent put together.

Consider the value here. If you allow yourself to set goals (not to mention goals based on purpose), you have an advantage over 95 percent of the population! The only question is: what do you have to do or be to feel worthy of goal setting and actualizing your goals moment by moment?

When you fail to plan, you are planning to fail. So, are you living a purposeful and inspired life?

Goals Founded on Lack

It is hypothetically easy enough to create specific plans with clear goals while still not feeling worthy enough to allow or to permit us to maintain the prosperity realized when goals are achieved. Those who place great emphasis on profit in business are in special danger in this regard. Many of them have the capacity, the will, and the courage to bring ambitious plans into action, but at the end of the day, they lack the character and substance required to enjoy and sustain prosperity. Their goals are founded on lack, impulses, and the when-disease. When the basis is greed and fear of lack, their plans cannot lead to prosperity. Even though they are dedicated to acquiring success, it is coming from a focus on what is absent. This will ultimately create the circumstance of lack.

Vision can be obvious and progress quickly and convincingly, but if fear and lack are the basis of one's goals and purpose, then there will be no substance to that progress—merely instinct and lack, which in the end will lead to absence, not prosperity.

If you do not allow progress to manifest according to the universal laws of cause and effect but try to push or force it forward all the time, there is no way for it to endure. You will always lack resolution because endurance does not comprise clenching one's fist but rather opening one's hand and allowing life to flow at its own rate. A discussion of endurance brings up the question, what is the difference between patience and impatience? Not very much, actually.

Impatience is the inability to entertain waiting, while patience is the ability to let time pass and suffer quietly. Life in prosperity does not involve patience. It has no suffering, no trials; life in prosperity is a continuous/ uninterrupted flow of light and love. The less resistance or struggle applied to processing in the moment, the less energy is exerted or invested in impatience/patience. The result is more resources to invest in the actual intention.

To endure means to last, and because there is no resistance in the now, endurance is maximized. The difference between being patient and being present is that when you're patient, you're waiting for something to happen, and when you're present, you have already arrived.

Goals Based on Impulse

Goals can easily restrict, maim, or send a person into absence from his or her existence when they are based on impulse rather than on purpose, when they concede to the when-disease. A goal without purpose is a check drawn on a feeling of emptiness that accompanies the completion of all projects—when all our energy has gone into finishing something and yet nothing has actually changed. Then the search for a new project begins immediately: "What can I find to occupy myself with now?"

Some people say, "Life is complicated." I disagree. I say that it is easy to live when your life is structured with goals and you are responsible for your existence and yours alone. It is easy to live when your purpose is clear. And when I say *live* I mean of course in the full realization of yourself—not simply getting by or enduring in the darkness.

We are talking about goals as dreams with deadlines. And you will see how wonderful and blessed it is when your goals have a purpose, especially when that purpose is noble and a true expression of your heart.

The Purposeful Use of Energy

The life of a ordinary person in a ordinary house comprises running between fires that he feels have to be extinguished immediately. Running in the direction of one of these fires, this regular guy is concerned about another fire that has already started to flame up too fast—in other words, he perceives that he has made an incorrect decision by attending to or managing the (wrong) crisis. The ordinary guy feels good when he has extinguished one fire or reduced it significantly and refers to his satisfaction by a big name . . . Happiness.

He calls his feelings happiness, yet this is crisis management and the management of chaotic power without purpose. Energy itself always has a purpose. It is always on its way to where it's intended, consciously or not. However, we do not arrange or order this energy ourselves; rather it is ordered and arranged by others around us by default. In this case, the purposeful use of energy is to be constantly on the run and chasing after problems, which has nothing to do with creating solutions. The only way to turn this around is by being responsible and purposeful and by directing the energy intentionally.

We have access to energy, but we do not want to be responsible for controlling it ourselves. Why not? Because, as we discussed in Chapter 3, the role of the victim is so familiar and easy to slip back into, and we do not want to be responsible for our own happiness or unhappiness. We would prefer to be preoccupied by extinguishing fires. We prefer to blame other people for lighting fires in our lives than to open our arms, grasp the energy, and decide to what ends we want to devote it.

I thought I could not be bothered to carry all the sticks to my own bonfire . . . and then burn them and burn them and burn them. Thus sang the Icelandic rock-and-roller Megas, describing brilliantly how we plot our own downfall—how we burn ourselves at the stake of guilt like witches, all by ourselves, on our own initiative. Why are we so invested in arguing for our limitations when it's just as easy to invest the energy in advocating our brilliance? Is it possible that we are emotional bookkeepers and that our self-image is reflected by how we feel about ourselves and this is what determines our self-worth? Is it possible that all we need to do is to love ourselves and then everything immediately transforms? My answer is YES! All you need is love, which is always the true foundation of purpose and a life of prosperity.

Your Life Is Never Without Purpose

So, what is the purpose of your life? If your answer is, "I don't know," then your current purpose is scarcity. When you lack something, it's because you're missing in your own life. If you do not know your purpose, your unintentional/unintended purpose is lack. Desire. Hope. Complaining. Self-pity. Knowing this, you have two options: to continue with that purpose or to choose to create a new purpose with intention, by choice, and using your power. It is an amazing moment in each person's life when they discover free will. That is the moment in which they become responsible. It is at that moment that a person becomes a creator and is no longer controlled by habit and automatic reactions. It is the moment in which we give ourselves permission to decide our own purpose.

Deciding your purpose does not require a revolution, just a change of attitude. It does not mean you need to quit your day job tomorrow or otherwise turn your life upside down. However, if you have allowed yourself to become bored and irritable in some situation, changing your perspective by refusing self-pity and resistance will get the light and energy flowing again. You will find increased strength merely by taking responsibility, showing up for the task at hand, and putting in some effort to direct the energy. A new perspective regarding your situation brings extra energy and increased power into your life—by simply transforming your attitude, the frequency emanating from you changes and that will spread to other areas of your life.

"I am"

My basic purpose is to do good and to understand that in order to thrive and prosper all of us must thrive and prosper. But when I first wrote down my purpose, I was a bit arrogant. My first version was as follows: *"I am a lighthouse that emits a powerful beam of light into the darkness, wherever I encounter it."*

Then several months passed. I thought about things and then revised my assertion: *"I am a lighthouse that emits a bright light."*

Another few months passed and in the end I wrote down the assertion that I have used since in one form or another: *"I am."*

My purpose today is not sacred or hewn in stone, but I feel at my strongest when I allow my light to shine for the benefit of others as well as myself, and I have full leeway and permission to adjust/revise my purpose if there is reason to do so. My experience of purpose is that it is always love and that it has no attachments—I just am. As soon as there are any attachments, I redefine the words I use to describe my purpose. At the heart of it, my purpose is always to be love.

Below are some of my personal declarations of purpose. When you're ready to define and declare your purpose, you can apply a similar format to various areas of your life. I do believe, however, that it is essential to sincerely gaze into your heart and examine your virtues and then define your values before you commit to your purpose. (Virtues are the intangible substance of values, and values are the soil on which you will build your new foundation.)

What is my purpose as a father? *"I love my children."*

Being a role model for my sons to turn to when they choose to do so. First and foremost, my purpose as a father is to understand that we are all different and that I must nurture my sons' options without burdening them with my will or impose what I want on them.

What is my purpose as a son? *"I love my parents."*

To learn appreciation for my parents and their contribution, and stop the blame game many children "play"—that is, being ashamed of their parents. To understand that I am not my parents, except to the extent that I invest energy and attention in the behaviors or traits that I either want or do not. That I choose whether I devote attention to the things they've taught me and I consciously decide to make part of my own values, disregarding the things I don't agree with. To behave toward my parents with love and sincerity, and appreciate (give them credit for) their contribution to my upbringing and development with no attachments.

What is my purpose as an employee? *"I am light and energy in my work."*

To respect and contribute honestly to the environment I work in. To devote my energies in such a way that my employer and I equally benefit. As an employee I am diligent and committed. I am inspired with a passion that I share with my working community.

What is my purpose with regard to my body? *"I serve my body in order to serve my soul."*

The body is the vehicle of the soul, and my purpose is to understand that my body is a temple. I approach it with the same care and respect with which I approach all that is sacred. My purpose is to serve my body so that I can be of service.

An Opportunity for Self-Examination and Growth

Language sometimes discloses deeper truths that always lay there but which we do not ordinarily see. I love to see the meanings of words revealed. For instance: *Intention. Attention.* These words are intimately related. They mean, "lean toward, reach for." They could not be clearer. Every word, every sentence, and the tone of your speech reveal your true intention. Every word and sound you utter serves to promote your self-image.

Gestalt therapist Terry Cooper once stated that if you want to get to know someone as soon as possible, all you really need to do is ask them the following question: *So what do you think about the government?* And then just sit back and listen to them disclose not only their views about the government but also completely reveal themselves through their perspectives, intensity, language, judgments, or praise.

All we ever talk about is ourselves and how we see things or how we feel and what we think about. Then we attract blessings or curses accordingly. The most powerful tool I have in my possession is to attend to my language and to tailor each word and sentence with a clear intention in mind. I also practice listening to what I say and how I say it with a great deal of attention, knowing that I am revealing my true self and my prosperity allowance each time I open my mouth.

Before I was liberated from the tyranny of the mind and learned to listen to and attend to my heart and its regular pulse, I was like a leaf in the wind. And strangely enough that is the description that many of my clients use when they first come to see me: "I feel like a leaf in the wind. I'm blown this way and that and land just about anywhere; I end up in many places that I never consciously intended to go to and doing things that I never consciously decided to do," one of them said sadly with a faraway look in his eyes, full of regret for time perceived as wasted.

"But how did you come here? Here to me? How did you arrive here and why did you come?"

"Well, I came here because I wanted to—because I want some relief from this suffering," he answered.

"Because you wanted to—of your own free will. You would never have found your way here without having been a leaf in the wind. You decided long ago to be a leaf in the wind—and allow yourself to be carried on the breeze of self-pity, without responsibility—in order to be able to point the finger at someone else and hold him responsible. You decided subconsciously to come here and in order to do what you had to decide of your own accord, for years on end, to be a leaf in the wind; you needed the wind to carry you into situations that hurt you enough to make you want to arrive here. Voluntarily."

The will was always at hand, unconsciously, unwillingly. And it is always yours. Always.

The consequences of the behavior to which you have subjected yourself, impulsiveness, and allowing yourself to be influenced by your hidden agendas can now be regarded as an opportunity for self-examination and growth. It is always your will. It will always become manifest. You are never without will. Your will be done.

The question is: Are you a reluctant passenger? Are you the kind of passenger who wants to be along for the ride, who never has any opinions about the itinerary, never content or pleased with the journey? Are you that reluctant passenger? Or are you the driver of your own vehicle?

Intention Requires Purpose

I am going to . . . but . . .
I want to do some good things with my life . . . but . . .
I am going to find a good partner . . . but . . .
I make up my mind to head somewhere . . . but . . .
I am going to . . . but . . .

When you remove the "but," your whole life will change. What is it in us that puts up fences as soon as we formulate our dreams—that locks us in, shackles us up, limits us, and reduces us? Why has everyone got a drawer full of dreams that have not come true and have become nightmares as a consequence? Why that *but?* The answer lies in these wise words:

> "Take your life into your own hands. What happens? Something rather scary! Nothing is anyone else's fault!"
>
> —Erica Jong

Purpose is notably the base of our behavior. However, purpose is not always clear and sometimes it is generated by negative and destructive intent. Our values fuel the reasons for our actions, consciously and sub-consciously. Values are not always positive, although we generally refer to them as such. How we view and value ourselves only serves to support our self-image and worthiness. For instance, the values of the criminal mind will reflect different agendas than the values of a mind focused on integrity and love.

By defining our values and purpose we are not only claiming responsibility for the energy we wield and our present state, we are also declaring ourselves a conscious creator. This is the role of co-creator of the universe. Without purpose, we elect to be passengers by default.

Creating by default is still creating. When we state intentions that we do not intend to follow through on, procrastination and self-deceit sustain our hidden agendas. We always have what is willed and thereby subconsciously wanted. This determines how we currently feel about ourselves and sustains how we will continue to feel about ourselves. Through procrastination and deceit, we dispense and invest a great deal of energy in distrusting ourselves and diminishing our powers. This behavior results in fatigue, fear, and distrust. Subconsciously the *imemine* governs our lives, and unless we tell the truth, become responsible, and restore our power, we will live in fear. We are so rundown by these behaviors that we are reluctant to be responsible for having been the cause of our misfortune. However, nothing that happens is anyone's fault. Life is always a divine blessing.

Many people have good intentions but no clear purpose. The difference between intention and purpose is that intention is often an empty and uncommitted announcement. It expresses an impulse, but not one that necessarily becomes action. It reminds me of the riddle of the three frogs: *Three frogs sit on a lily pad. One decides to jump into the pond. How many of them are left?*

The answer is, of course, *three*. That one frog merely made a decision to jump . . . BUT . . . he didn't do it. That is what happens to so many of us. We make the decision but . . . Whenever I tell this riddle to a group of people, it is rare that someone has the correct answer. We do not detect the difference between making a decision to jump and actually jumping—because we are so deeply embedded in our own patterns of behavior. We are too preoccupied and enthralled by our addictions to negative behavior patterns to notice that we are chasing an illusion. We continue to serve the *imemine*. In this way, intention can cause us pain because we are always kicking ourselves when we fail. Each self-betrayal counts, and the emotional expense is high. It's a setup. If we do not love ourselves, then subconsciously we are intending to succeed at failing.

"If a work is incomplete, it is at least begun." This assertion may well be true. As soon as we commit ourselves to a written and dated goal that is founded on purpose then we have already embarked and come a long way. But . . .

But what is the reason for all these half-finished tasks and projects? Could we be repeatedly rehearsing our intentions only to betray them? Our lives are full of "good" intentions about improving ourselves in various areas of our lives—get ourselves in better physical shape, have more communication with our family and friends, clean the car more often, read more. The list is endless. If someone really intends to get himself into better shape and takes the first step by purchasing an annual membership to the gym . . . why does he decide to quit after three months?

There are two reasons for this:

1. Insufficient permission. We only do what we believe we have permission to do. That permission is based on our capacity to accept love and prosperity. No one exceeds their own permission—it is the key to prosperity.
2. Undefined purpose. As soon as I record why I want to go to the gym regularly I begin to do it—when the purpose is clear, when the purpose is love, when there is a genuine purpose. Going to the gym on the basis of lack ("I want to look tough or cool") will not last long and will absolutely not increase either the amount of love or freedom in my life.

When we write down precisely our set of goals and give them specific dates, then we will achieve them. A wise man once said that a goal was a "dream with a deadline." That sounded eloquently phrased to me and still does.

When we have understood that awareness and attention are love, which is light, and that ours is the power and the responsibility, then we are infused with inspiration and a passion to bring our own purpose to light—to decide and choose.

How do we experience this inspiration? By deciding what we truly want and therefore being responsible for manifesting what we want instead of what we don't want. By making ourselves available to love and prosperity, opening our hearts and lungs and allowing the cosmic energy to breathe through us, inspire us. We consciously make ourselves available to prosperity by breathing deeply and rhythmically to infuse our intentions. What happens when we breathe deeply? We consciously ingest oxygen from the atmosphere and our lungs begin to expand, full of inspiration and also full of space. If the body is a furnace, an energy transformer, then it constantly requires inspiration in the form of oxygen to sustain the flames of passion—then the heat will be great and the smoke thick. Then expression will be intentional, strong, hot, steaming—purposeful.

Motivation Versus Inspiration

There is a clear distinction between motivation and inspiration: Motivation is always based on lack and is always attached to a conclusion (reward) or a destination. It is always an attempt to escape from the pain of the past, avoid the present, and grasp the mirage of future happiness. To be governed only by motivation is to be constantly absent.

Inspiration, on the other hand, derives from being creative in the present, by enjoying the present moment, placing the journey above the destination. William Shakespeare understood this completely when he composed one of the most famous lines in all literature: *To be or not to be, that is the question.*

Man's absence has many different manifestations—general consumption of food and drink, physical and emotional imbalance, compulsive obsessive behavior, and procrastination. However, one of man's most salient absences is the pursuit of goals that lack purpose. There, we see when-disease in its most vicious form—it is here that one is always chasing after something.

To be or not to be

Creator or accident
Empowered or powerless
Complete or incomplete
Willingly or unwillingly

The choice is yours
Yours is the power
You are the power and the glory

A goal without a purpose is like a juicy carrot. And carrots are the donkey's favorite, as well as the *imemine's*. This is because while the carrot is being chased, the *imemine* is given a very long leash and grows stronger. Finally obtaining the carrot usually does not render the happiness that was *hoped* for, which further encourages the growth of the *imemine*.

Purpose is the foundation for what we do. Do we want to hope and whine instead of creating purposefully and responsibly? On what basis do we formulate our actions? Do we want to go to the gym because we think we are overweight? Do we want a relationship because we are lonely? Do we want to be in business because we desire wealth? Do we want to enter politics in order to gain power or the respect of others?

What are we going to do after we lose weight, become rich and powerful, and are no longer lonely? What then?

When our actions are motivated by emptiness and lack, our self-image is projected by insecurity and fear. When fear and lack become the base of our creation, fear and lack are what we attract and manifest. The moment we acknowledge our current state and embrace and love ourselves, the essence of our creation changes from scarcity to prosperity. When we love ourselves anyway, our self-image emanates love not fear!

If I Were Sure That . . .

Many people chase after goals that are either devised by others or substantially influenced by others, regarding their content and formation. But what if you ask yourself this question: "If I were absolutely certain that I could not go wrong, what would I do? If I could do all that is necessary to get there, what would I want to do?" When we answer these questions, we can take a look at what it is we use to hold ourselves back. Is it fear of failure or is it fear of success? Either way, if fear is the motivator, then shame, regret, and remorse are the foundation of your creation. You are always right: how you view and see the world is your prerogative and can never be wrong—your perspective rules. Fear does not have to be your motivator if the foundation of your purpose is love.

Arriving in the Valley of Shadows

Once we have shrugged off our illusions through the experience of becoming conscious, we find ourselves in no-man's land: the valley of shadows where we are neither motivated by greed nor inspired by purpose. There is nothing new about this idea, and you may recognize this in a different context:

> *Yea, though I walk through the valley of the shadow of death, I will fear no evil: for thou art with me . . .*

Although these lines are from Psalm 23, we all know what this means. A similar idea can be found in all religions. When we step out of the illusion, we enter the valley of the shadow of death. There we have neither inspiration nor are driven by motivations or enticed by things to reach our goals. We see the truth of the illusory, and we also see the path of illumination. And we know in our hearts what will serve us.

When our eyes grow accustomed to the dark and we have oriented ourselves, two paths that lead out of the valley appear. On one side is the rock face of motivation. It is steep and difficult. At the summit is a wide perspective with a view far into the distance. It is hard to ascend, and not everyone can manage it. The rock face is a familiar task: it is the painful process we call ordinary life, the struggle that we are trained to take on. Reaching that summit is thought to be a time to rejoice and revel in the glory. It is the driving force of all ambition—to win, to conquer, to dominate. However, it is cold up there. We want to get to the summit, but we do not want to stay there. Why struggle to get to a place where we do not want to stay?

Life is a challenging business—including so great a series of difficulties that we should be applauded, awarded medals and cups for going through with it at all. *Life is a vale of tears. No pain, no gain. Whatever doesn't kill you makes you stronger.* And so on. Society has found a plethora of ways to tell us that it is natural to suffer. But a person in the valley of the shadow of death can no longer cope with that belief system. She no longer believes in the suffering. She has often been cut and bruised making her way to a high summit without finding any happiness and without discovering any greater light than on the flat ground below.

On the other side of the valley lies the second path: the smooth slope of inspiration. Here is a path we can take to stride out of the valley slowly, calmly, effortlessly, one step at a time, and in all probability that we will enjoy the walk in the end, imbibed the beauty of our surroundings and the light, arriving 100 percent safe and sound at our destination.

But the person who has newly emerged from the fog of illusion does not know how to walk along the smooth path on the easy slope. She has never done that. She does not believe that this easy path will bring any happiness. She does not believe that the path to light and happiness is so straightforward. And until she believes that, she will continue to dwell in the shadows of illusion, and if she does that for long enough, she will exhaust herself for good and all—or design a new motivation, a new carrot to chase, a new cliff to climb.

Conceivably, that new motivation will be demanding, preoccupying, and distracting for the mind, and when we reach the top, nothing has changed. The motivation was the carrot and we hankered after it like a donkey. Happiness is not at the summit, nor at the end of the rainbow. So where does that leave us? In the valley of shadows where motivation is on one side and inspiration on the other.

How do we move from being motivated to being inspired and passionate? How do we infuse every cell in our bodies so that they illuminate like the very first rays of the sun, that each second of our lives is kindled by energy, awareness, and gratitude for being here at all—to eat, sleep, love, kiss, laugh, and cry?

How do we establish a protocol? How can we change our perspectives so that each day we are buoyant, smiling, strolling into the bathroom, looking in the mirror and touching our hearts with one wink—by just gazing in our own eyes and feeling love for what we see? By allowing ourselves to be fully present in the valley of shadows. By not wanting to leave, by loving all that exists, and by loving being present even in the valley of shadows.

Why do we want to cross the valley of shadows, when in fact the perception of the valley exists only inside us. The moment we are fully present and enjoy ourselves, then the energy is present, light radiates in the valley, and the darkness recedes. Then we can see clearly and choose our next step.

Be your own sun, your own guiding light, your own glow. You can do this by eliminating years of self-pity, by choosing not to be a leaf in the wind, by celebrating the fact that you are *responsible*, by deciding your own purpose, *by turning on the light, and by embarking on the journey.* Without a new set of premises (without deciding your own purpose), it is not possible to illuminate the valley of shadows.

This is the most important decision you will ever make, the greatest conceivable confession of love. This is your decision that you are the light that ought to be shining at nothing less than full strength.

Using Affirmations to Support Change

Every time I have wanted to change something, whether in my behavior or my perspective, I have used affirmations. I write them down on a piece of paper and then begin to express them. My first reaction is always resistance—the *imemine* always reacts harshly to my quest for prosperity. Resistance reveals that I have only limited permission since making such assertions always requires extended permission.

I reiterate the affirmation often enough until it eventually tunes in to the frequency of my heart—until my heart sanctions the affirmation and begins to broadcast it at full strength. This may sound a little grandiose, but in fact this method is not unlike breaking in a new pair of shoes. There may be places where they pinch or are uncomfortable in some way, but with time, they almost become a part of you.

Affirmations are constructive, specific declarations that help you to direct your awareness away from self-sabotaging, negative behaviors and affirm what you truly want. To affirm is to act. They help you clarify and believe in what you're constructing and affirming to yourself. Affirmations are tools that serve as the framework required to establish new beliefs and behaviors. You can use affirmations at any time, in any situation in which you are intending to create positive change. For instance:

- Shift your awareness from feelings such as frustration or anger and direct them toward love and compassion.
- Improve your self-image and worthiness.
- Stay on track and honor your commitments.
- Inspire or improve productivity and effectiveness.

The power of affirmations is greatly enhanced when founded on purpose and performed in conjunction with S.M.A.R.T goals. Once you've identified the goals you intend to manifest, you can use affirmations to inspire yourself and sustain your resolve.

Affirmations greatly enhance the effectiveness of visualization. When envisioning the change we intend to manifest, we're also verbalizing the intended outcome aloud, using a supportive constructive affirmation. There are many ways of affirming constructive changes. Some use affirmation CDs, cards, mobile apps, or daily reminders by email, computer screen, and sticky notes to remind themselves to affirm.

I prefer writing my own affirmations in direct relation to the changes I am instigating. For instance: "I command prosperity and affluence, and I am happy, healthy, loving, sincere, kind, caring, and generous."

Once you construct the affirmation, I suggest writing it down in your notebook or journal. The more often you affirm your statement, the more powerful and affective it becomes. The affirmation becomes a rudder for your intentions. **All that you devote your awareness to prospers and thrives**. Once you have established your intention on paper, I suggest you express it mentally and verbally.

Write an affirmation that best describes your intentions. Always begin the statement with the words "I am" or "I command."

Accomplishments Without Purpose

I know a highly accomplished man with an impressive résumé of achievements. Whenever he has conquered some peak or other, he finds himself without purpose. I encountered this man at a restaurant and have seldom seen anyone looking wearier or more depressed.

"Why are you feeling sorry for yourself?" I asked him with a grin.

"Gudni," he said. "I have achieved all my goals. I've just come back from the climb of my life."

He had invested a great deal of time and energy into climbing one of the highest peaks in South America; indeed, he nearly killed himself in the ascent. He was a long way from his wife and children while he undertook this task of passion . . . and what was the outcome? He missed the journey and found no happiness when it was over. There was no climax.

When we embark upon a journey or undertake a task not founded on purpose, we are likely to miss the journey even though we may reach the alluring destination. We are only motivated by achieving the end result. When the reward of completing a goal or a project is an illusionary promise of grandeur or the hidden agenda of becoming good enough "when" I reach the top, then the lack and emptiness that propelled you to the top will reemerge once the high or exhilaration of completion wears off. On the other hand, a goal or a journey founded on purpose is inspired and actualized moment by moment.

Toppling the Pile of Bricks with a Smile on Your Lips

Do you remember playing with bricks when you were small? Do you remember piling them high into something beautiful, like a castle or a palace or a ship, concentrating and sure of what you were making? And do you remember when you discovered that what you had built was actually quite unstable and with no secure foundation or put together wrongly or simply just ugly and you needed to knock it down and start over?

You just did it.

The same thing applies to waking to consciousness in your own life, being responsible and choosing your purpose, defining what you want to build with your bricks. It just seems a thousand times more complex and proves to be very difficult for many of us, among other reasons because we have forgotten the endless possibilities of what we can do with the bricks, and moreover, we have forsaken the freedom and the will to decide what we want to use them for. This is a dream we are all familiar with.

At the same time, we often experience a mixture of fear and respect when we hear of someone who has changed course in life—for example, a person who has always been successful in business who changes gears completely and decides in middle age to learn gardening or open a health food restaurant.

Some of us are filled with gladness when we hear this kind of story because we know that it was the right choice in some way—perhaps we also feel a certain degree of envy and resentment because we also entertain a longing to do something similar but do not believe we can. We become frightened by our acceptance of the inability to shake off old patterns of behavior, frightened that we could/can never topple the pile of bricks and build on a new, more secure basis.

Why can't we face the fact that we have taken a wrong turn? Why can't we acknowledge we've been chasing a carrot, that we've become what we are on the basis of negative feelings toward ourselves, that we've survived on the lack that characterizes the *imemine*? Do we just want to chase carrots? Where does that chase end? It can end now if you are prepared to change your perspectives, define the "why" of your actions, and enjoy the journey, savoring each moment.

Showing Ourselves Love

A few pages back I talk about arriving in the valley of shadows where I refer to Psalm 23, The Lord Is My Shepherd. This psalm is a promise to God and an announcement by the person who recites it that he trusts the Lord to protect him, stand beside him, and look after him. Can we trust ourselves that way? We can when our purpose is clear. The psalm would then become:

My psalm

I am my own shepherd,
I shall not want.
I make myself to lie down in green pastures,
Lead myself beside the still waters.
I restore my soul.
I lead myself in the paths of righteousness
for my name's sake.

Yea, though I walk through the valley
of the shadow of death,
I will fear no evil
because I am with me.
I prepare a table before me
in the presence of my enemies.
I anoint my head with oil.
My cup runs over.

Surely, goodness and mercy
will follow me
all the days of my life.

And I will dwell in my house
for the rest of my life.

I am my shepherd.
I shall not want.

While you might think this brings about a radical change in the meaning of Psalm 23, know that there is nothing outlandish about restoring our own souls, allowing ourselves to rest, being our own shepherds, leading ourselves to still waters, or following the paths of righteousness. It is a sign of healthy self-love and a healthy view of ourselves. It is a sign that we have respect for ourselves and that we shall look after and support ourselves. It is a sign that we understand the eternal rules: The respect that others have for us will never be greater than the respect we bear for ourselves.

If we live on the basis of lack and absence, we have trouble thinking about ourselves, embracing ourselves, and showing ourselves real love. Being unable to do this and turning to other people to look after us and for things to bring us happiness is a sign of a deeply ingrained pattern of dependent behavior. We are choosing to be dependent on the idea that other people give us a sense of fulfillment—whether these "other people" are friends or family or even God.

And despite this dependency on the idea that others are responsible for keeping us safe, many of us also believe the old adage that a man designs his own destiny. And that brings us back to the valley of shadows. Here, just like there, there are two options. On one hand, there is the idea that someone should be taking care of us and on the other hand there is the idea that it is all in our own hands. These two options tend to frighten us. Why?

In the first place, we are frightened of the idea of God. We are so used to thinking of ourselves as grains of sand in the great sea of eternity with no power because a supreme being decides our fate. This frightens us even though we may not even think we believe in God. In the second case, we are frightened of taking our lives in our own hands—frightened of taking responsibility for how we feel and for our own progress or destiny.

So far we have neither any real trust in God's looking after our interests nor in our own creative power over our lives. We have been neither one thing nor the other. Not quite on this side and not quite on the other. Just in the middle. Somewhere in between. And that is not a good place to be.

We avoid taking our lives into our own hands and avoid trusting a higher power at the same time. That is simply a battle between dependence and independence—we refuse to believe that we are merely victims of our own circumstances, but we also refuse to take responsibility for those circumstances. We distinguish between these two views and cannot see that they are connected. They are connected because I am God and God is me:

> God is the best possible version of myself.
> God is me when I shine with freedom.
> God is me when I am light.

None of this has anything to do with organized religion. When all is said and done, these two ideas may be combined. I can place myself in the role of God, as perceived in traditional religions. I can lie down if it is good to rest. I can restore my soul, be my own shepherd, stand beside myself, protect myself, and prepare a table in the sight of my enemies. I can trust myself so much that I am ready to face my enemies.

We cannot trust God if we cannot trust ourselves. We cannot believe in God unless we believe in ourselves. We cannot have faith in others unless we have faith in ourselves—not until we show by our actions and deeds that we are ready to raise ourselves to our feet instead of kicking ourselves when we are down.

At that point, we will really become our own friends, the one we rely on most. Our purpose will then become crystal clear. We will be our own creator in full awareness and bring to light all that our heart desires. In this way, we can have relationships with other people without attachments. In this way, we can love ourselves fully and with the greatest light. Thus, we become the leaders in our own life, our own shepherd.

> Believe in two
> The majestic source
> Creator of all
> And the creator within
> —Steingrímur Thorsteinsson

Purpose Overrides Your Imemine

The *imemine* exists in the subconscious and is extremely powerful and devious. When you have no purpose and do not have goals based on that purpose, it drags you with it wherever it wishes to go, from one temptation and distraction to another, from one punishment to another. The *imemine* thrives in shadows and darkness, but it has great passion and an iron grip. To maintain the suffering that is darkness and rejection, the *imemine* concentrates on the lack that is most challenging and difficult for you—those areas of your life where it identifies emotional charges sufficient enough to insure adequate suffering and anguish.

The *imemine* thrives on ingratitude because it is not possible to experience absence and be grateful and illuminated at the same time. Those two never exist at the same time. Therefore, the *imemine* is often attentive to things you (think you) do not want, whether they are wrinkles, a few extra pounds, the rubbish in the living room, or the rust on the car. There is plenty to choose from. No one wants to be as they are. Everyone is worried that they are not enough or that they do not have enough.

Worrying is praying. That is why people manifest what they are preoccupied with and regularly receive what they *think* they do not want. Suffering issues from this frame of mind: we direct all the light at the pain, at being overweight or whatever else we do not wish to be. It is from this attention on absence that pain is born, *absence being the mother of all disease.*

One exercise I use in my workshops is to have the participants draw a line on a page and write down all they do not want on the left side and all that they want on the right side. Then the piece of paper is folded into two with the "don't wants" facing down.

This is a simple way to direct our attention at what we want rather than at what we lack in life. And strangely enough, it is considerably more difficult for people to fill the right margin than the left. Writing down what they don't want takes no time at all. They know it so well.

We have been conditioning our attention and directing it to the things we don't want for so long that we hardly know any longer what we do want. We are much more familiar with what we don't want—and by constantly directing our attention to those things, we will them toward us. We water and nourish the green grass on the other side of the stream and it flourishes. It is essential for us to become responsible and acknowledge that what we have is what we have willed thus far. Then, we must take action by declaring our purpose, making S.M.A.R.T. goals and becoming the drivers of our own vehicles, masters of our destiny.

Contemplating Purpose

All that we accomplish is based on purpose. This is an unavoidable universal law. Purpose is the end that justifies the means. That is why we must seriously contemplate the meaning of purpose. Ask yourself these questions:

- What values govern my life?
- What am I interested in?
- What holds my attention?
- What are my intentions?
- What influence do I intend to encourage in the environment and myself?
- What do I want to achieve in life?
- Is my life today based on my purpose?
- Is my life today inspired by a desire to create my own destiny and to exert influence on the world?

These are big questions. You can answer them when you have obtained permission from yourself to ask them, when you permit yourself to place a question mark against how you have lived your life so far.

My goal is not to change in an instant the lives of everyone who reads this book. It is my sincere conviction that each person's purpose is to discover his or her own free will—to be empowered and to obtain full permission to organize his or her own energy and life according to their own values and ideas—to stop living like a victim.

We understand that our lives always have a purpose—energy is always being invested whether we are aware of the fact or not. We understand that it is our role to decide on our own purpose and that until then we remain victims, *imemines*, and irresponsibly without conscious intent. We decide our purpose and announce it openly. Purpose produces goals. Goals are dreams with a deadline. We commit ourselves to achieving these goals. And then we proceed to go to work on them immediately. We set off from where we are and make our way toward a life that is inspired and infused with passion.

> **All that you devote your awareness to prospers and thrives.**

And that is how the light is kindled, and it continues to burn—not only when the goal is achieved but for the whole journey—all the way, in each small step, each second when all goes well and also when you feel things are not going well. When we have purpose to ground ourselves and a clear goal that is based on a vision, we can deal with any challenges or obstructions that may stand in our way. Then we can manage all the ups and downs of the journey in stride—and enjoy it. It's from the twists and turns that one learns—to show us how in the endless now.

When we have purpose we do not pronounce judgment–we simply enjoy the journey of our existence. A journey founded on purpose is one without attachments and expectations, where the steps are taken in trust and in pleasure along an even path. A journey without expectations can therefore never disappoint.

We understand the idea of unconditional love, especially when we are talking about our children: "I love you and will always love you, whatever happens." This is love without attachments—unconditional love.

Looking at life as a journey without attachments sounds like this: "I love being and living—I love all that takes place because that is how it's supposed to be. Everything is as I intended it to be. I love the journey that is life."

Purpose Is Your Version of Love

Purpose is the foundation of all affluence and prosperity. Man's purpose is always love; what distinguishes us from one another is the manner in which we define *how* we love. Your version of how you love is your purpose. You choose how to devote your energy and express your love in the world. A goal founded in purpose is a statement of gratitude. A goal based on purpose is constantly experienced and actualized in the present moment. Every moment you experience joy and personal contentment in your own skin. You *want* to be as you are now. You never regret or repent anything you have done in the past.

This is life when the *imemine* is no longer in control. It is not possible to rid ourselves of the *imemine* entirely, for it lives deeply entrenched everywhere in our beings. However, it is possible to place it in loving exile (suspended animation) and diminish its power considerably. We love the *imemine* just like all that lives within us, but certainly not enough to listen to it. We love it. With light. That is the only thing required.

Seek and Ye Shall Not Find

We neither need to "search" for a purpose nor "find" one, but we can in any given moment *decide* what our purpose is and then clearly define it. Everyone's purpose is to be fully responsible for his or her own free will and to be fully present and empowered in his or her own existence. Although the purpose is always the same, it can assume many different guises. The content of the purpose is always the same: to share yourself, to love, to inhabit an idea of "us" and not of "me." Purpose is the essence of being in unity and service—not separation or absence.

If you are searching, you are lost. You are not present with yourself, here and now, as you are now. There is nothing to find except yourself. If there is a lack or absence in your life, you are lacking or absent from your life. When you feel there is something missing, it is you who is missing—you are not present in your own life.

It is exciting to be present. When we awaken into awareness, we are empowered and can choose to be responsible for our own existence and thereby release a huge amount of energy that we have invested in the sins of the past, self-pity, resentment, regret, and remorse, in searching for ourselves, for meaning, and for happiness. Then we can claim energy as our own and invest it in the present and the purpose that we identify with. We are pure energy, souls, light, love. How we invest and devote our energy—how we choose to exert our energetic influence on our environment through the roles we assume—is the great opportunity.

Place yourself in a quiet harmonious mode and ask your heart the following questions:

- What is the premise of my existence?
- What role am I acting out today?
- What role do I want to play?
- What do I want?
- Why do I do what I do?
- What if my life right now is as good as it will ever be?
- How do I intend to work things through?

When Is Enough Enough?

Consider this: if happiness is to be found in achieved goals, why is it likely that we haven't stopped and thought to ourselves, *Hey, I am pleased at what I have achieved so far, and I don't need to search any longer. I am all that I want. I am a fulfilled human being. I have all that I want. My life is perfect. I am complete.*

Why, after all this searching for fulfillment, happiness, and peace, are we rarely ever able to feel like this and when we do we are only able to enjoy or sustain these feelings for more than a brief moment? Could it be that our basic premise has been wrong? Is it possible that the following universal law applies: *He who searches and searches may not find anything—but if he stops searching he will discover all manner of things.*

There is a great deal of difference between searching and being open to discovery. He who is searching for something reveals a lack—an unspoken declaration that he is not sufficient in himself, here and now. But whoever understands the heart is the emperor and there is only light and love is light, and he is solely responsible for his experience—he experiences a purpose by listening to his heart.

And then he can set out happy—with purpose, wholly aware and abundant with love, with full permission to enjoy life with himself. He can feel his own presence and he can feel life. He is complete.

Purpose is the rudder of happiness and the premise of inspiration and passion. We are fully responsible for our purpose or lack thereof. When you intend unconsciously, you disperse energy by investing it in resistance. Creating by default always has consequences and the energy allocated, even though it's devoted unintentionally, is an expense invested in what you think you don't want, but actually do want because you are always responsible for the energy you wield through your thinking, acting, or being. Free will is the tool of awareness and responsibility. When you intend, you choose, and it is in awareness that empowers you by the forces available to you each moment. Presence is power because you are fully aware of the consequences instigated by your choices; you are therefore a conscious creator with a clear purpose.

Where We Are and Who Brought Us Here

Awareness and responsibility are the first two steps. Awareness is the light that is love and compassion. There is nothing except light and love—all else is the illusion of the *imemine*, the pastime of a wild creature that does not want our light to shine because it would lose its power over us.

Responsibility is to be present in the only thing that is true, the only thing we have or have ever had—the present. Responsibility means being fully responsible for being here, right now, being responsible for our own energy, our own deeds, and our participation in what happened in the past, regardless of whether that is pleasurable or emotionally challenging. Responsibility is being present here and now, being present, empowered, and ready to take charge of our own life and state of well-being. To be present and assume the power invested in choice, to be present in order to choose to respond, not to react unconsciously on the instinctual principles of the *imemine*.

What happens after these first steps? Purpose. Purpose is established. Who decides our purpose? We do. How? By giving ourselves the space and the liberty to listen to our heart. Purpose trembles in the frequency of our heart, but the noise in our head has prevented us from ever hearing it properly. Even so, we know and have always felt, deep down, what our purpose is.

The first three steps shed light and enable us to discover our own free will—so that we can be empowered. They prompt us to decide on our own path. We have free will and power to invest our energy as we wish—in absence or in prosperity. The choice is entirely ours. We alone are responsible for whether we enter the darkness or walk in light.

daily reflections

Ask yourself the following questions and record the answers in your notebook or journal.

What do I want? *Each of us knows what we think we do not want; however, most of us are reluctant to declare and document what we do want because we subconsciously know that by doing just that we must become responsible and take action by making changes. This is frightening to us in the light of the permission we feel worthy of. What you want is the premise of any journey or mission; otherwise you can't change direction or chart a new course. Write a detailed description of what you want.*

What is my role in life? *What role are you playing now? Are you the lead actor in your movie or just a stand-in? View your roles and write out the role you envision and want to play.*

What is my contribution to life? *The surest way to get is to give. Document your gifts and how they can benefit and empower you and others.*

Where am I? *What's your current situation? Take inventory—emotionally, mentally, physically, spiritually, financially, and socially. Write down how you feel about your life now and become responsible for having brought yourself there. Use this as your starting point. The beginning is always now.*

Where am I headed? *What is your mission in life? Have you embarked on your life's journey and how are you doing? Write a short assessment.*

What is my vision? *Are you able to see clearly your heart's desire and how it unfolds? If not, what's required to enhance clarity?*

What is my purpose? *Write down a purpose statement. Begin with the words, "I am."*

Commitment

Acting with Integrity from the Heart

"Commitment means that it is possible for a man to yield the nerve center of his consent to a purpose or cause, a movement or an ideal, which may be more important to him than whether he lives or dies."

—HOWARD THURMAN

Commitment

is the holy grail of trustworthiness and prosperity. The moment you commit yourself, the universe takes you seriously and your permission to flourish is maximized.

Step 4. Commitment

Commitment is a decision to move in accordance with the world, not against it. It is the rudder of purpose, a way to stay on the right path. Commitment is a declaration of worth and a statement of intent. It involves allowing ourselves to open and trust the heart and the will. It is a conscious decision to be fully present. Commitment is a covenant with ourselves to stand by our word, keeping our promises to ourselves and to others. It is when we finally commit to ourselves that the universe takes us seriously and begins to work with us in conjunction with our stated purpose and goals.

Commitment is to commit to yourself and honor your own purpose and goals. This step fuses the heat of awareness, the joy of responsibility, and the resolution of purpose. Commitment is the Holy Grail, the blessed vessel of prosperity. Commitment is an agreement forged by the heart, a sacred covenant. When you keep your commitments, you are trustworthy. When you live in accordance with your commitments, you unify and strengthen your character.

Our word is sacred and by keeping our word we fortify our trust in ourselves. Through our commitments or lack thereof, we subconsciously maintain our self-image and prosperity allowance. By committing to someone or something, we are giving our word, promising our loyalty to a purpose, task, project, cause, or another person as well as to ourselves. This way, we feel worthy to receive and sustain love and prosperity.

Commitment is a declaration of integrity, a promise made from the heart; it is the adhesive that sustains our resolve no matter what happens. Commitment is the only language providence takes seriously. Until our intentions are committed within the unity of the heart, they are solely based on the duality of the mind.

The heart is the emperor, knower and ruler of all. Anxiety constrains the heart and prevents it from reigning in peace, but when the heart has full space to beat, it clears away all shadows.

What does it mean that the heart is the emperor? It means that the heart runs the show. It beats as long as the energy of the body lasts, it contracts and expands, and it sends sound waves and electrical impulses into the body's energy system, the soul, and the whole world. Our limbs dance to the sound of our heartbeat, and every single cell in our body hears the song. The heart understands the world before our senses perceive it, and our brains respond to its myriad stimuli. The heart broadcasts on a frequency that sends out a clear message about what we feel we deserve.

> The heart is the emperor.
> The heart is light.
> The heart is all there is.

When we commit to our heart, we redefine ourselves, resign our membership in the societies of absence and victimization, and commit ourselves to a new role in life: To be the messenger of love and the bearer of light.

As soon as we concentrate entirely on our central task, we force an agreement with the universal essence, the sacred energy to which we all belong. In that instant, the universe begins to take us seriously and offers us its cooperation. When we commit to something, we are not only promising ourselves and others, we are also making a covenant with the sacred, combining our energy sources and strengthening our connection to everything with whom we have a relationship.

Commitment Gives the Heart Space

We all understand space. We all understand the committed heartbeat and the natural rhythm of contraction and expansion. The heart pulsates with all the power it has, but daily abandonment and confinement suppresses and/or restricts its power. We restrict the heart's ability to pulsate naturally. Our heart will not "attack" us unless we betray, reject, or abandon it.

Commitment gives the heart full space—space to simply be and to permit miracles to take place, space for all that is, space that obeys its own laws, space with a purpose that amplifies the message of the heart and resounds throughout our daily lives. The power that emerges from committing to the heart makes us worthy and permits us to create the space required to receive and metabolize the energy of abundance—without causing spiritual, emotional, or physical indigestion.

Commitment to Truth

The truth is love and light—complete fearlessness in harmony with the frequency of the universe. In his book, *The Last Lecture,* written at death's door, university professor Randy Pausch pronounces famously, "If I could only give three words of advice, they would be, 'Tell the truth.'" I have three more words to add to that: "All the time."

The truth illuminates our existence. Illusion disappears; the *imemine* goes into permanent hibernation. It retreats into the shadows when light begins to stream forth again. This happens when we are attentive; when we feel responsible for our own existence, well-being, and emotions; and when we understand that our sacred task is to have purpose with goals. When we make a commitment to being on the same frequency as our heart, the shadows retreat without struggle and the whole heart can express itself with full power and beat at its own natural pace.

When we are present, the heart understands that everyone's perspective is always right, that everyone has the same right to experience what he or she is experiencing and that all is as it should be. When we are present in our own heart, we see through illusion.

Fighting the Laws of Nature

All diseases originate from constraining the pulse and rhythm of the heart. The heart beats naturally in joy, and when we constrict it with rejection and falsities, we are fighting against the laws of nature. We do not allow for contraction and expansion, the ebb and flow of all living things.

Anxiety is stored up as doubt and fear, which restricts the space of the heart. Doubt is as far from love and light as it is possible to be. It is the longest and the hardest distance of all. But we put so much faith in doubt: "Yes, what if someone attacks? The world is so cruel . . ." We are used to wanting to protect our heart and shield it from perceived threats and danger. In the vaults of experience, there is abundant evidence indicating how cruel this world and people can be. But the greatest cruelty is what we do to ourselves. That is why we do not trust anything—the world, other people, or ourselves.

This threefold distrust is an illusion like so many other things. The only distrust that matters is that we show ourselves. When we do not trust ourselves, it doesn't really matter what the world is or isn't or how others behave toward us. All of that becomes secondary. Whoever inhabits the present moment and trusts themselves welcomes and celebrates all life and loves the world at large. He doesn't need constant self-judgment or self-deprecation.

But . . .

"But . . . what if?" says the *imemine,* pointing to its own hoard of experience and regrets, which it uses to sustain itself. "What about doubt?" says the creature of distrust and lack. It can sound very convincing indeed. Along with the understanding that we are the light, are responsible, have purpose, and have made a commitment comes the understanding that this "but" is only the *imemine*'s method to maintain illusion. The illusion dissolves when we refrain from devoting energy to the *imemine* and listen instead to our hearts. Feel how much less energy you expend when you are not trying to maintain a complex illusion.

Verdict

I stabbed you in the heart with the verdict
so sharply that
the wound closed up

you will not die, I said
but you need to downscale
the way you lead your life
that will actually be easier
than you think
a little like
downscaling your apartment

you'll be surprised how much is dispensed with
without regret or consequences

Though I know, it will be hardest
to sever links with those who long ago
attached themselves to your generosity

But if it works then you will see
that this disease was long due

—Ari Jóhannesson

Commitment Opens the Heart

All healing begins in the heart. That is where life is. That is where the present lives. That is the dwelling place of generosity, gratitude, and trust. The consonance/harmony of the heart with honesty, truth, beauty, and justice is the only path to peace and prosperity—the only path into the light and a life with purpose.

Commitment allows your heart to open. You tear away the plastic packaging and protective wrapping and experience the heart as emperor, allowing all doubt and fear to dissipate. You then trust your own will, existence, and purpose. This is the core of awareness.

When we are not fully present, we are always doing things halfheartedly—allotting our own existence and surroundings a limited portion of prosperity and thereby actually allotting absence instead. Commitment, on the other hand, is a sign that we are promised to ourselves, wholly and completely, through thick and thin, up and down, and inside out. We are perfectly empowered in the present moment and show up fully and tell the world who we are and what we want. We become the designer and leader of our own lives, just as some of us are prepared to devote ourselves to another person forever in matrimony. Oddly enough, we commit ourselves to other people, dedicate ourselves with ambition to our jobs, and we commit to protect our children and kin at all costs. Yet we hesitate to promise ourselves to ourselves, through thick and thin, in sickness and in health, till death do us part. Denying this, our credibility is gradually sacrificed, and we begin to distrust ourselves. Why do we commit ourselves to someone else before we have the might and the permission to commit ourselves to ourselves?

Commitment to our own life and person is no more complicated than committing ourselves in marriage. It contains exactly the same principles and structure. Yet our commitment to ourselves is even more important. A commitment ceremony where you promise yourself to yourself is as simple as saying:

"In love and joy, in the eyes of the world, I promise to share my life with myself in every second. I vow to be devoted and true to myself. I will

support myself through thick and thin. I will walk with myself along life's path. In my name. Love. I vow to commit myself to myself and promise myself eternal support and love in all my actions, great and small."

Commitment means signing on the dotted line, marrying yourself with all of your advantages and faults, come what may. There is no instruction manual, no blueprint. The formula is always the same:

All that you devote your awareness to grows and thrives.

To commit to yourself is a decision to sow the seeds of devotion and gradually permit yourself to put down roots and grow:

I love myself anyway. Whatever my appearance, whatever I do. I will always love myself. I love myself anyway.

Your happiness is always in complete harmony with your permission for happiness. We are as joyful or happy as we permit ourselves to be. And by sowing this seed and permitting yourself to grow, you immediately increase your prosperity allowance. The way to increase your permission is to love yourself and forgive yourself and thereby reclaim the energy you had invested in ingratitude, disappointment, shame, regret, and remorse. The next time you love yourself despite having "made a mistake," you expand your permission even further, and so it continues.

A Story About The Woman Who Could Not Conceive of Loving Herself

I conduct workshops on energy and restraint in which we examine our nourishing patterns and the attitudes that lie behind our consumption of food. For a number of years, these workshops took place on the weekends.

I remember one woman particularly well because she taught me a lesson without actually intending to. As I looked across the group, I noticed her immediately because I could sense how doubtful and critical she was. I thought, *She won't turn up tomorrow.* I immediately dismissed this negative thought and told myself, *Of course, she'll come.* Then I put aside this distraction and continued with my lecture.

And what do you know: the following morning, there she was again. I was very pleased, but she devoted the whole day squirming about in her seat, obviously bothered by something. When the second day of the workshop ended, I thought again that she probably would not turn up the following morning. Again I dismissed the thought. I did not want to prejudge her or project myself onto what I thought she might be thinking.

On Sunday the last day of the workshop, the woman arrived again. Yet she was not the same woman at all. She glowed, smiled, and joked around with the others. Her shoulders were relaxed, the restlessness had disappeared, and she no longer had her arms crossed. I sat down beside her during the lunch break and asked what had happened.

She smiled and said, "I slept poorly and was feeling awful. I simply could not grasp this idea that you were constantly hammering away at. The idea that this is where I have arrived and I have myself to thank, not to blame, and that I am fully responsible for where and what I am, that I should love myself. Then, last night something happened. I was lying awake in bed and turning this idea over and over in my head—that I could not love myself. That was too much, too selfish, too egocentric. I just couldn't, and I was not going to come again today."

"Yes," I said. "So what changed your mind?"

"Lying there, wide awake, it suddenly occurred to me that if I couldn't love myself, I could at least commit to being my friend. I *wanted* to be my friend."

Her thinking could not come to terms with the idea that she wanted to love herself, but eventually her thinking "admitted defeat," and she found a direct route to her own heart: a path into a new existence where she chose to be her own friend and to honor that friendship. Her dissatisfaction with herself had been such that she wasn't willing to love herself until she had reestablished her faith and trust in herself. She understood that by reinventing her relationship and befriending herself, she could gradually forgive, open her heart, and embrace herself and eventually love herself unconditionally.

An Open Heart Touches All Things and Needs No Protection

The *imemine* constrains the heart with doubt, temptations, grumbling, procrastination, lies, betrayal, trickery, remorse, regret, hope, whining, resentment, apprehension, fear, and the when-disease. All of that creates a thick protective layer of insulation that mutes the rhythm of life that the heart emits in love. The chest, upper back, and shoulders become a breastplate, a shield. However, the moment you fully commit yourself to full cohabitation with yourself and are fully responsible for being the creator and leader in your own life, your heart beats without limitation and you transmit a powerful message to the universe—a message that clearly states that you are now fully responsible and committed to your relationship with yourself and your life.

Commitment tears away the armor plating around the heart. With no shield, the heart pulses with amplified power to the world and to all that live in it—an open heart touches all things and the world begins to move in accordance with it. The world begins to listen and move. When commitment removes the constraints surrounding the heart, allowing for vulnerability and the exposure the heart yearns for. It fully trusts its own power and the light that dwells within it. An open heart needs no protection—just the freedom to shine its light and transmit its frequency at the greatest possible power.

What universal principles support this? An open heart is just love and light—and when I love with all my heart, then I am not in the "I" or "me" mode of thinking. Then I understand that I am *us*, that everything is us—and therefore I have nothing to fear.

Contentment comes from freeing yourself from the straightjacket of the *imemine* and sharing yourself with the world, to give gifts—not to tighten your grip on them. Contentment comes from allowing the world into your heart and allowing your heart to open to the world.

From glowing awareness the will to be responsible is born. The consequence is that you are fully empowered to govern your life. Responsibility produces the permission to define your own purpose—to stop being a leaf in the wind. All of this creates the basis for a life of prosperity. Commitment is a decision to be fully present in your own life in the now as you are without attachments, resistance, judgment, or prejudice.

Commitment is looking out from the heart, sensing the vibration in purpose, envisioning your desires, projecting them on to the internal screen of your existence, and commencing the journey. By committing yourself to your purpose and goals, you create a continuum in your life—in harmony with the vibrations of your heart. When you commit to your purpose, your purpose becomes a dependable rudder that will keep you on the right path. When you lose direction, you choose not to blame or punish yourself and will fear nothing because you know that your purpose will steer you in the direction you need to go. The goal is being actualized in the moment—in the journey, in the motion that is always.

In your heart, you always know where you are and who you are, and therefore, you trust that all is as it should be right now.

The Heartbeat of the Chicks

A nature documentary once showcased a species of bird that always flew to the same shoreline each year to build its nest, lay its eggs, and raise its young. An aerial shot of the shoreline showed hundreds of thousands of birds, squawking and screeching all day long. In this species, it is the male that looks after the chicks while the female flies out to sea to search for food. She returns at night with her beak crammed with food and then begins to look for her mate and young.

Imagine the scene: the beach crowded with hundreds of thousands of birds that all look exactly the same. Just imagine the commotion. How does the female bird find its nest? Does it have such a powerful GPS system that it can see and remember the exact location of her mate and chicks before she set out? What if they moved during the time she was away? Does she have such incredible hearing that she can distinguish the squawking of her mate and chicks among the cacophony of screeching around them? Or can she sense the frequency of the heartbeat of her chicks who are completely in tune with her own? Some say that God programs them and others say they locate each other by the sound or the frequency of the voice, rather than by sight. I am convinced they find each other by instinct, sensing the vibrations emanating from heart to heart.

Reexamining Discipline

Commitment requires discipline. That's an annoying word, isn't it? *Discipline*. We have strong views when others attempt to get us to be more disciplined; yet we have a mixture of respect and fear for those we consider self-disciplined. We respect them but are perhaps a little envious of them. As a result of that envy, we may even find ourselves belittling disciplined people by suggesting they are somehow denying themselves the pleasures of life, having swapped them out for the constraints of regimentation.

However, *discipline* is one of those words that we want to reexamine to question some of its traditional connotations. To be disciplined means to tell the truth, commit ourselves to something, and be there for ourselves and others when we have promised to do so. To be disciplined means to honor our word, which is sacred. When we commit ourselves to prosperity, our permission for prosperity increases evenly and surely. Then we can exercise our discipline as it should be exercised—with love.

Commitment is the essence of discipline and order. Telling the truth and honoring our word is the premise of self-control and restraint. To do what I say is the most powerful way I know to establish my faith and reliance on myself. By honoring my word, I exercise trusting myself and thereby reinforce my essence. When we exercise our discipline with love, we don't go to bed early because we are forcing ourselves to, for example, but because we understand cause and effect: when we stay up late we are responsible for being tired the following day. We embrace this responsibility and do not complain—and that's why we go to bed early with a smile.

Embarking on this journey is often the most challenging step. When we decide in our hearts to take the path of integrity and depart from self-destructive behavior, the *imemine* comes out snarling. It is used to having its own way and will fight with all its might. There are turning points. Again and again, we find ourselves at a crossroads in life. It is rare that we take a new path. We are so conditioned and addicted to our current behaviors and belief systems and so emotionally wired by our habitual patterns that it requires a major life occurrence or breakdown in order for us to lift the spell of the *imemine* and proceed into the light and follow the purpose of our heart.

If you are at a crossroads, ask yourself whether you want to hear the truth, tell the truth, and live the truth. The truth opens the way for the greatest possible expression and provides the heart with ample room to pulse. Those who do not want to surrender and release the grip of the *imemine* are resisting structure or boundaries just as they resist being responsible and committed in their lives with great intensity. In between, with great suffering, it is possible that we may take a step toward greater prosperity, but until we have managed to say, "I love myself all the same," we will not have earned any more permission to seek prosperity. Searching for it without permission will result in fumbling and grasping at air.

We do everything we can to avoid discipline and the structure required to create miracles—until such time as we believe ourselves to be worthy. We will not release our grip on suffering, punishment, or being spellbound. We choose not to cross the threshold of suffering into the region of prosperity and tranquility before we give ourselves permission with steadfastness and discipline. We can choose another way. We can choose to make a commitment with integrity and carry it through with discipline.

Commitment, Integrity, and Discipline

Commitment comprises light, promise, discipline, and persistence. Integrity means that we trust ourselves to be credible, believable, and to stand by our word. We believe in ourselves and trust ourselves because we give ourselves full permission for prosperity. This makes us trustworthy. Discipline simply means that we honor our word, both to ourselves and to others. When we keep our commitments often enough, we establish more self-trust.

Commitment is best described as making a covenant—we tell the truth. Commitment is the premise on which the universe receives a clear message of my intent, purpose, and goals. When we stand by our plans, we trust ourselves and our own strength and become worthy creators. This increases our worthiness and therefore our prosperity.

My mother-in-law once called me an extremist. I was amused and asked her to explain what she meant. With a mischievous smile on her lips, she replied, "You are the only man I know who stands by everything he says." My mother-in-law was right. I am an extremist because I fully commit myself. I don't believe in doing anything half-heartedly. I don't subscribe to "maybes" or "later." I believe in the full expression of my potential. In order for my expression to glow and radiate, I must honor my commitment, be present, empowered, and fully responsible for how I choose to devote or invest my energy.

Behind the Door Is Light

There is a door in all of us, and behind it is a light. At first we have no clue that it is there. Then we hear of it or we begin to suspect that such a door exists. Then we catch a glimpse of it through the mist, the dust, or the darkness. We wonder for a while whether we actually believe what we are seeing and whether anything good lies behind the door. We might think the door is not intended for us but for someone more deserving, someone who is not as incomplete as us.

But, eventually, if our intentions are pure and we honor our word, we do see the door clearly. And at some point we believe it is intended for us. Then we take a small step toward it—inch our way forward, one step at a time. Some of us get far enough to be able to stand next to the door. Some even get to put their hand on the door handle and discover that it is all true: there is a door here, and it can be opened. Others go a little farther and open the door slightly and see the light coming from deep inside. And then do nothing—they just stand in a dark room and let a little light shine on them. However, those who want to be illuminated, who are free of the spell of the *imemine*, who understand that they always have free will and can choose their own response and purpose, who believe in their own power and their own light, they tear the door open with all their might and then bathe in the light. A miracle. A matter of heart.

If I Ingest It, It's Love

My commitment concerning nutrition is simple: "If I ingest it, it's love." So, generally speaking, I eat wholesome, live, and organically grown food. I enjoy it with awareness, gratitude, and love. I chew it well and eat in moderation; otherwise, I exceed my body's metabolic capacity and create digestive difficulties that diminish prosperity.

Having done this for a long time, I know my body very well. I hear when it calls out for food, but I sometimes detect a different kind of invocation, an invocation to absence. That's when the *imemine*, as quiet as a mouse, suggests to me that I eat and drink just to fill myself. It doesn't ask for an organically grown apple or herbal tea. It wants a lot of food—a good juicy steak and a soda too.

Usually, I feel worthy enough to give the *imemine* a friendly pat and thank it for its suggestion. But occasionally I do what the *imemine* suggests. I allow the creature to get a hold on me and then I gorge myself in a way that serves both lack and discomfort.

That is where the commitment comes in. When I nourish, it's love. I don't kick myself when I'm down or suffer in shame and humiliation over "cheating" on my principles about healthy food. I do not shame myself or feel guilt if I bite into a hamburger and put some ketchup on my fries. I love myself. I love myself despite everything. I love myself even when I'm down, and I help myself to my feet. It is in such circumstances that small miracles take place. The unhealthy food that I ingest stops becoming a way to punish myself.

The same can also be true for others: A few years ago a man who was HIV positive came to see me at his wife's request. He had only a few minor symptoms at the time. I talked to him at length about how he could build up his strength and balance and stressed that he needed to take the initiative and cooperate with me because neither his wife nor I could do it for him.

Although he listened with interest and seemed receptive, he did not make the changes he needed to make. He was not committed.

When I saw him again a year later, he was very ill. I welcomed him back, paying little attention to his apologies and embarrassment, explaining that it was better for him to be ready to make the commitment, despite his deteriorated condition, than to approach my suggestions halfheartedly. We started to work together, and I saw that he was in bad shape both physically and psychologically.

When I asked him what he thought was the worst thing about his condition, what caused him the greatest challenge and discomfort, he replied, "The medication! It is poison! It tastes like chemical waste, and I have to drink it every single day! I try to reduce the bad taste by mixing it with fruit juice, but I get nauseous after I take it. I have no appetite, and I'm a wreck."

"Not so complicated. We'll sort this out," I said, to which I received a look of surprise. I explained, "I'm not going to do anything. You're the one who is going to change this. Now, listen up. Medication is the 'elixir of the gods.' Thousands upon thousands of people have been working for decades, inventing, discovering, developing, and producing these drugs. And a vast number of physicians have tested them on thousands of patients. An immeasurable amount of energy, manpower, and money has been invested. Everyone who has been involved in developing and producing that concoction has done so out of a sincere wish to help and to save human lives. I can assure you that if you open your heart and bless the medication and bless all the people concerned for their contribution, the outcome will be entirely different."

The man looked at me in amazement after this lengthy speech and then he said, "I think I know what you mean."

Two days later, he came back to see me wearing a wry smile. He explained his good cheer: "I gave the medication my full attention when I took it, blessed it, and those people involved for wanting to heal me," said the man. "And I haven't felt nauseous for two days. I am full of gratitude."

From that day onward, his health began to improve. It was not the medication that was poisonous, but rather his disproportionate resistance to the medication. Instead of fighting against it, he let go of his resistance and gave it his blessing so that the medication could be used at full strength in harmony with his personal frequency.

Understanding Our Place in Nature

At some point we are each confronted with this simple question: Do we trust the universal laws of existence?

We trust that the sun comes up each morning and nourishes the flowers and the trees and seals and worms with its beams. We trust that thick banks of clouds usually mean rain and that the ebb and flow of the tides is connected with the gravitational pull of the moon. We trust that nine months or so elapse between conception and birth of a child. We trust in all this and subscribe to all the laws of nature. Why, then, is it difficult to trust that our purpose is to live in peace, light, and prosperity? Why do we want to believe that the destiny of man is to be stressed, anxious, frightened, rejected, envious, merciless, codependent, angry, bitter, greedy, regretful, disappointed, destructively critical, violent, and cruel to other people and to the world at large? Why would we trust there is harmony and balance throughout nature with the exception of humankind?

Is it possibly because fear, lack, and doubt have been leveraged to govern and motivate human behavior for millennia? Is it possible that our animal instincts of fight and flight are so ingrained that our reactive impulsive behaviors dominate our lives? It has been stated that the average human is approximately 5 to 10 percent conscious and that most of our existence is governed by the unconscious-subconscious impulsive behavior—what I call in this book the *imemine*. This means that awareness is the key to transformation.

Once we awaken, we have access to free will and can choose to be responsible for sustaining awareness and the energy we wield. This energy can then be consciously and purposefully invested in prosperity. Commitment is the essence of the moral compass governed by the laws of cause and effect. Our degree of commitment to our purpose is the genuine reflection of our self-worth based upon our self-image and therefore our prosperity permission. We can only give what we have, and love and prosperity are synonymous just as commitment and integrity are the substance of generosity—generosity being true prosperity.

Commitment originates in the heart. When commitment is founded on a true sense of worthiness, we tap the intelligence of the universe where all the information about living a holistic and enlightened existence exists. Then, for the first time, we have permission to access that information and live our life accordingly.

Commitment means empowering our own light—strengthening and expressing it. Commitment is being liberated so that we have free will and the conviction that we are empowered to choose love and peace. Commitment is allowing the heart to provide us with the strength to turn the corner and dare to proceed into the unknown.

Because the heart is the core.
The heart is the sun.
The heart is the core of the sun.
An open heart is unlimited love.
What is there, then, to fear?

daily reflections

Ask yourself the following questions and record the answers in your notebook or journal. (Your response can be as simple as yes or no. If no, also answer why not. If yes, answer what that means and looks like to you.)

Is my word sacred?

Have I fully committed myself?

Have I committed fully to my life?

Have I committed fully to my purpose?

Am I living from my heart or my head?

What permission do I have at this moment to be prosperous?

Am I a brightener or a dimmer?

Am I loving life?

Advancement

Progressing with Love and Permission

"You are the power and the glory.
What you believe is what you create.
That is what you become.
Thoughts are energy.
However, thoughts are powerless
until you are present
and infuse them with purpose, passion,
  and commitment."

—GUDNI GUNNARSSON

Advancement

is expressed and projected by the frequency of the heart. Every thought, emotion, gesture & action is the sacred dialogue of abundance.
To will is to act.

Step 5. Advancement

Advancement (or progress) is the materialization that follows the preceding four stages. Once we become aware, have assumed responsibility, determined a purpose, and committed ourselves, we inevitably discover that everything begins to fall into place. Advancement is born of harmony. With clarity of intent, we begin to create our future and manifest our destiny. When we devote our awareness to a specific purpose, we become responsible for what we create. Any image, word, or action that we conceive of will begin to materialize according to the emotional intensity, passion, and awareness we invest in it.

The only way to measure support or supervise our progression is by creating and following the blueprints of prosperity. Remember the old adage *When you fail to plan, you plan to fail.* When there is no strategy, that's the strategy. The boundaries you define and the structure you construct around your purpose, vision, and goals will provide the strength, measuring tools, and guidance (in other words, the blueprints) that are required to stay on a forward-moving track. I am not just referring to the blueprints or the goals themselves; they are merely the outlines and the directions. I am referring to the company you keep, the dialogue you use with yourself and others, and the practices and routines you create to substantiate your commitment to the journey.

Keep in mind that everything we do reveals our true intentions to the universe. At the same time, our actions speak clearly to ourselves about what we truly feel comfortable obtaining, having, and enjoying. By placing ourselves in the dialogue (or the environment) of progress and greatness, we are influenced by that structure. For example, if someone wishes to be more spiritual, progress will be made if he or she regularly partakes in a spiritual practice in a supporting environment. Spiritually based rituals are conscious practices that promote the framework of intent just like affirmations and other actions do. Structure your prosperity with loving discipline and communicate your worthiness with clarity.

Actions Speak, the World Listens

To will is to act. Our worthiness and our intentions are revealed in the way we express ourselves; the world listens and does all it can to support and validate our self-image and statements of intent—whether we ask for prosperity or scarcity. Show me your friends, and you have revealed yourself. Show me, too, how you live, how you nourish, and how you dress yourself—because we broadcast this information to the world with our every breath, every heartbeat. We are energy transformers, and we constantly transmit our heartfelt committed intentions, consciously or not. The information about our expectations, whether we feel worthy of prosperity or lack, is defined by how openly the heart expresses itself and by the vigor and self-assurance in which our posture, language, and emotions communicate. How we view ourselves is always revealed and cannot be hidden from fellow hearts.

It is very clear we are not our thoughts, our attitudes, or our opinions. What we create is what we believe—and what becomes of us is directly connected to what we ask for. Our affirmations, actions, and awareness are self-perpetuating and self-fulfilling prophecies. Consciously or unconsciously, we become what we ask for. Our prayers to ourselves are heeded.

One of the most important questions we can ask ourselves is: "Is the world a friendly or unfriendly place?" This gem is attributed to Albert Einstein, but there is no proof he ever asked this question. For our purposes, it does not matter whether these words are his. They are valid. Equally compelling is the question: "Do you see the world as friend or foe?"

What are your beliefs about the world? Is it a friendly or an unfriendly place? Do you perceive the glass to be half full or half empty? Or do you see and understand that "my cup *always* runneth over"? Answering these questions brings awareness to how you perceive the world. Our perspectives govern how and what we communicate. What we believe and how we view things determine the story we promote and the roles we play. We constantly look for evidence to prove ourselves right regarding the beliefs to which we subscribe.

Henry Ford famously said, "Whether you believe you can or whether you believe you can't, you're probably right." Keeping with this theme, my favorite quote is "Whether you argue for your inadequacies or your magnificence, you must provide the evidence." Trying to prove oneself right preoccupies the *imemine,* and there is no logic at play. The programming is just a survival mechanism based on the information to which we have subjected ourselves. Our actions are completely instinctual until we awaken and become aware of our patterns. Whatever you believe is what you become. This is why natural miracles take place when we change our perspective.

To will is to act. If we are not taking action, we are not allowing progression. The opportunity at hand in this step is to observe our behaviors, which reveal our true self-worth and self-image, and then use this information to make necessary adjustments to allow continued advancement.

The Framework for Natural Miracles

When we feel we are worthy of prosperity, our hearts, our bodies, and our whole lives express it. We abandon impulsive, habitual behaviors and become conscious and responsive. We adopt intentional patterns of behavior that support the intentions of the heart. This is advancement.

Allowing ourselves prosperity and full expression has two requirements:

1. Purpose—a clear, committed, and powerful vision outlining the goals that illustrate what we want to create.
2. A heart that is open to receiving whatever gifts support our inspired vision.

Then comes the framework required for the miracle. We create it and endorse it, again and again, continually progressing toward our goals with purpose. That might sound a little unromantic or in opposition to heartfelt ideas about the magic or mysticism of miracles. Of course, we want some things, such as romantic love and miracles to be beyond reason and analysis, but miracles come not from some outside force but from ourselves.

Let's look at the word "miracle" itself. It means something to be wondered at, marveled at. But one of the Greek words consistently translated into English as *miracle* is the word *dynamis* or *power*, later becoming *virtus* in Latin. This is what the word means—but we are used to seeing miracles as coming from some outside force, something that God or some higher being initiates and which has nothing to do with us. But what if we decide to put the *dynamis* and the *virtus* back into the miracle? What then? It is possible that if we feel worthy and use a well-organized framework we will permit ourselves to live in prosperity? Can a miracle be constructed and organized? Yes.

A miracle is a change of perspective, a change of attitude. In its most beautiful expression, a miracle is a different way of experiencing things. Let's enter a new existence where we admit that the power is within us to consciously intend our miracles. When we are purposeful, committed, and completely invested in our tasks, we consciously manifest miracles.

Allowing Ourselves to Advance

We can only advance as far we allow ourselves to go. We want to apply new practices, perspectives, and lifestyles that are tailored to prosperity. We want to condition ourselves with permission and compassion. We want to do this with discipline that shines and confirms our love for ourselves and our existence. We need a framework. However, the *imemine* is always on the alert and ready to pounce. It is usually most successful when we do not have the structure of clear intention and purpose. There must always be some kind of conscious plan. If there is no plan, the *imemine* will take immediate advantage of the situation.

The *imemine* is very limited; it does not know how to enjoy life or to find happiness in the present moment. Organization and planning are its nemesis. Any framework restricts the *imemine* even further since it wants free rein. A disorganized existence will render it the greatest amount of freedom. The only occasion on which the *imemine* agrees to a framework is when that framework entails such constraints that it is almost suffocating. To shake off old habits, we need support, a plan, organization, and refuge—that's the way to get past the *imemine*.

Changing a Prayer of Disparity to an Affirmation of Love

A while back, I was on automatic default. I had allowed my energy to become depleted, and I began to recite an obsessive prayer of disparity: "I am poor, lazy, unhealthy, unhappy, full of hatred, ungrateful, stingy, overweight, powerless, and imperfect." That's an intense accusation—the song of the martyr! Such a song of desolation can play on in our ears for years on end if left unchallenged, making us feel even worse. However, with many years of physical and spiritual training, I have changed the way I conduct myself and choose the affirmations I allow into my mind when I have invested my energy in absence, exhausted myself, become bored and tiresome. The affirmation sounds like this:

> *"I am prosperous, diligent, healthy, happy,*
> *compassionate, grateful, generous, lean, empowered,*
> *sincere, and complete—and I love myself."*

Now you have an opportunity to do the same: Take a deep breath, exhale slowly, and center yourself. Take out your notebook or journal and review your declaration of intent. What do you want? Next, review your purpose statement and use the inspiration and enthusiasm evoked by your purpose to fuel your vision. Now write an affirmation beginning with "I am" or "I command" that clearly states your intentions. Edit it until you feel empowered when saying the affirmation aloud. Begin now, be bold, and create the magic you envision.

Let's take a look at the progress we are making in our lives. We make sure we fix all leaks and stop all gaps before the rains come. We encourage our children and help them until they can make their own way without us. We use slings, casts, and crutches if we break a limb. And when we plant fragile seedlings, we place them in an environment conducive to their growth because we know that with the right conditions they will thrive. If we leave them to themselves, they may be adversely affected by a number of variables. Those fragile plants may wilt and die. Just like all else that grows, plants need attention, nourishment, love, and protection. Why should different laws apply to self-nourishment and growth? When we dispense with the behavior patterns of the *imemine* and take the path to prosperity, we also need nourishment, a framework, and refuge.

How is it that we understand the need for protection and shelter in nature yet refuse ourselves those supporting conditions when we move away from the shadows and into the light? Are we denying ourselves a natural right? Are we sabotaging ourselves? Unfortunately, the answer is most often yes. We hold back and restrain our forward movement literally by creating tension and resistance toward advancement. This is because on some subconscious level we do not feel worthy of progression and don't trust ourselves enough to wield the energy of prosperity. We are subconsciously afraid of hurting ourselves and others by attracting energy or opportunities we don't feel worthy of or trust ourselves to process or handle.

How you express yourself reveals your worthiness. How you truly feel about yourself is always transparent. When there is little or no advancement, look at how much entitlement you have rationed yourself. Contemplate and strategize what changes or adjustments are required to progress or even exceed your current permission. What actions are required? What steps require revisiting so that you may enhance your glow? The moment you allow yourself to relinquish the behavior of victimhood, scarcity, and lack, your advancement will unfold without force.

Constructing the Framework

Just as crutches are used for temporary support, the framework you construct need only be temporary. You will not require support for the rest of your life. But while you free yourself from the spell, it is essential to create a framework that supports and strengthens your new lifestyle and diminishes the level of stress and interference in your immediate environment. A framework means having documented specific, measurable, attainable, relevant, and timely goals. A framework means keeping track of your nourishing patterns, especially within the context of your spiritual and physical well-being. A framework means always being responsible emotionally and never making a victim of yourself. A framework means choosing to be around people who think along similar lines or who at least have an understanding of the changes you are advancing toward. A framework means making a decision not to take it personally when others make discouraging comments or belittle your commitment to change.

A framework comprises all this and much more. And it is easy to construct and maintain such a framework after you have made a decision and committed yourself to prosperity. Blueprints and strategy are the framework for implementation and progress. In Chapter 3, I discussed declaring our purpose and inspiring our vision. Vision thus became the design of the S.M.A.R.T. goals we documented—goals that we intend to actualize moment by moment while thoroughly enjoying the journey and keeping the destination in mind. In Chapter 4, we committed to ourselves, our purpose, and to prosperity. In Chapter 5, we implement these goals by creating the strategy required for actualizing our dreams and desires.

We are constantly expressing ourselves, revealing ourselves, and conveying to the world how worthy or unworthy we feel we are. The change consists in expressing ourselves within a new framework and from new perspectives—in committing ourselves to a changed perspective to advancement because then the world will come to our assistance. They say, "God helps those who help themselves." Of course, we know that faith moves mountains, but sensible people have advised us to take a shovel with us, just in case.

A framework is a *plan* for prosperity. A goal founded on purpose is actualized in the moment, not at a destination point, just as a framework for prosperity is not prosperity itself. We create a framework for a miracle, a framework for change, a plan that will act as protection around us while we are putting down new roots. But just as a plant ultimately needs to stand strong against wind and sun, so we need to eventually dispense with our support mechanisms to live life fully.

It is also possible to lose yourself in the framework and allow it to change into fetters and constraints. What is the difference between having a support mechanism and being constrained? A framework provides faith and is built on love while constraints come from mistrust and doubt. Nothing truly creative can take place while constraints remain. The same difference applies to a true leader and a micromanager. The micromanager always distrusts and uses all kinds of constraints—physical and spiritual—to maintain his position and his control, while a true leader employs a framework to delegate and allow the maximum amount of freedom and creativity.

A framework is a compassionate structure to hold things to together and provide support. It is a way to conserve strength and not always expend it on just keeping ourselves afloat. It is a way to circumvent constant decision making, weighing and measuring, and self-questioning.

Life becomes simpler with a framework, and after a short while, a miracle will take place within the framework—the child will start to walk on its own two feet, without help. The child begins to walk when it believes that it can—when it trusts itself to do so.

Pulling the Plug on Habits

It has been said that it takes about three weeks to break any habit. To create a new regimen, we have to rid ourselves of old habits by literally disconnecting them from their source of energy within us. That does not happen of its own accord, but it is actually a simple process if we allow ourselves time to retrain ourselves and implement new behaviors—just like when you buy a new pair of sneakers that give you a blister the first time you wear them but eventually shape themselves to your feet and become indispensable. The task is to create a support mechanism around a new plan in which we feel worthy of prosperity.

Have you ever bought an annual membership to a gym, and then stopped going after a few weeks, and then beat up on yourself for quitting? This repetitive punishment is the *imemine*'s favorite sport. Why does this happen again and again? There's a very simple explanation: *We abandon our plans because we do not feel worthy of prosperity. And as a result, we deplete our worthiness even further.*

We have not allowed ourselves to live in prosperity. That is why we constantly renege on our intentions, betraying and abandoning ourselves at those moments when we think we are ready to change our lifestyle (to stop smoking, stop drinking alcohol, stop eating fast food, and so on). Perhaps we do believe that we want to live in prosperity—but we do not believe we *deserve* to. We have not given ourselves full permission to do so. Not actually, not for good and all. When we stand there with a credit card in our hand and buy an annual membership to the gym, are we truly ready? Are we prepared to see this all the way through? Or are we buying a year's membership on false premises? Are we doing it because we have low self-esteem ("I *have* to do something to get rid of this extra weight") or because we are susceptible to the opinions of others ("I can't go to the beach this summer looking this fat")?

There is a great difference between doing something because we love ourselves and doing it because some external view or opinion persuades us that we *ought* to do it. This is the great divide—I can never be fully worthy until I am prepared to say with all my heart: "I love myself anyway."

> *I am 50 pounds too heavy—I love myself anyway.*
> *My apartment's in a real mess—I love myself anyway.*
> *I'm having trouble making ends meet—I love myself anyway.*
> *This is who I am now—I love myself anyway.*

By deciding to love ourselves, we are forgiving ourselves; we are letting go of remorse and the befitting self-punishment, revenge. We open our clenched fist and put away the whip we have been using to flog ourselves. Our behavior reveals our true feelings of worthiness. Only by taking action are we confronted by our limitations. When they appear, either we choose to love ourselves anyway and thereby increase our self-worth and self-image or we choose to reject and abandon ourselves only to perpetuate the same patterns or vicious cycle of blame and punishment. The only way to advance and achieve lasting change is to love ourselves anyway.

It's a double-edged sword. You cannot increase your worthiness before you create a support mechanism, and you can't create the framework before you give yourself permission. So, what would suffice to begin with? That the seed of worthiness is within; when you use that seed to create a framework for new behavior patterns that serve your purpose, then prosperity has been aroused.

Forcing Progress Is Not True Advancement

Have you attempted self-coercion in order to get yourself to complete a task or endure an experience? When you force progress, you can be certain of one thing: you are going to sustain some cuts and bruises. There's even a danger of seriously injuring yourself.

A lot of people I know live their lives like this. They face life's slopes and peaks, their eyes full of doubt, despising what they are about to encounter. They do not actually want to make the climb at all, but they feel they can sense what it's like at the top. All they can see is the summit, and they feel like they are compelled to make the ascent. Then, after having focused obsessively on the top, they clench their fists, assault the slope, and try to claw their way up.

That is not true advancement. It is being obstinate or hotheaded and will result in harm. Many people are really stubborn and can continue like this for extensive periods of time, edging forward with the handbrake on all the way. They are trying to run into the future but are tied to the past. This takes sheer obstinacy. It is driven by the *imemine*, which thrives on confrontation.

Progress requires endurance, which is effortless with its purposeful flow.

It means having the presence to advance slowly—not with clenched fists but with an open heart and the ability to be present and thankful for the blessings on hand in the moment. It is enjoying the journey, not fighting it. True advancement is progressing gracefully, knowing that the destination can only be experienced in the now. However, if you feel like a reluctant passenger, then you are a victim or martyr held hostage within your own nightmare and the only option is to awaken and take responsibility and thereby lift the spell with love.

Becoming Worthy of Achievement

Offenders who have done time in jail report that, for most, being released back into society is a major challenge. They report that after having been in prison, they need to adjust to being free. Only a few can bear the light, especially just after being released. This is the reason why so many offenders return to the constraints of a penitentiary. It is easier to fall back on old habits then it is to overcome challenges and adjust to the light. This is a game we all play, but we are each spellbound in different ways. What is the psychology of the repeat offender? Why do we seek out the safety of restrictions? Why are we so reluctant to take responsibility? What does it mean to be addicted to our negative and destructive behaviors—to be an alcoholic? Or a nicotine addict? Or a shopaholic? Or a distraction junkie? It means to be captive, spellbound, or incarcerated by behavior patterns and emotional/psychological constraints that we have imposed upon ourselves—enchantments that we sustain and even reinforce.

How we choose to be absent or constrained is an individual affair. Do you use food to sustain your absence or your suffering? Alcohol? Drugs? Sex? Tobacco? Disease? Sickness? Lethargy? Romance? Shame? Which of these substances or behaviors are emotionally charged enough to keep you from being present?

The practical use of these questions is to bring your subconscious patterns to the surface so that you may become aware and liberate the energy devoted to sustaining an unconscious identity. Remember, there is no wrong or right in the realm of energy—only cause and effect. When you say you want change, you must act and then be different by directing your awareness to that which supports advancement rather than what detours it. Answer the above questions in your notebook or journal. Detect if there is an emotional charge when you answer. If so, energy is being invested in holding back. If you choose, you may invest this energy in advancement.

Advancement requires intent to create space for light in your life. If you rush out of your own darkness, the light might blind you—you get stunned and freeze to the spot or retreat quickly back into the comfort of your own incarceration. We are so used to the dark, so used to a dimmed and restricted existence, that we need to build up greater receptivity to the light. Advancement is that opportunity. We allow ourselves to progress and change our perspectives and our story about ourselves. Moving out of our comfort zone with love and clear intentions in the form of purposefully envisioned and committed goals is permission-based advancement. This is progress based on love; it is true prosperity.

The way we express ourselves in the language we use, our presence, and our behavior reveals how worthy we are of advancement. Worthiness can only be enhanced by becoming trustworthy through keeping our commitments and honoring our word. And that is how we gain forward momentum.

A Tale of Resistance and Procrastination

What is top on your list of boring things to do? My answer would be cleaning the floors at home or washing the car. These are both tasks that I endlessly postpone and that always make me irritable and impatient, which is absurd because I naturally want my home and my car to be clean. But of course, the matter is much simpler. Why do I hate doing the floors and cleaning the car? Because I am boring while I am doing it.

I carry out all kinds of mental gymnastics. First, I procrastinate for days, sometimes weeks on end. Then I begin to chastise myself for having a dirty car and for not taking more care of it on a daily basis, and then I feel sorry for myself for having to do this menial chore. I would much rather use the time for something creative or to read or jog or just take it easy.

Before I go and clean the car, I am seriously resistant to the task. So I stretch things out as long as I can (and of course, by this time the car is really filthy). While I wash it, I am still resisting and derive no enjoyment from it whatsoever. My self-pity only comes to an end when I have completed the task. Then I have a small moment of freedom and am immensely proud of myself for having carried out "mission impossible." But this moment of triumph is short-lived. The next phase follows immediately where I promise myself that this will never happen again and that I will take better care of my car and not let things mount up from now on.

And of course, I do not do this. So the next time I manage to force myself to clean the car, I can once more start tearing strips off myself for not having kept my word.

Procrastination is an amazingly powerful tool to ensure that I never live life to the fullest. Resistance has many different roots and can appear in a thousand guises. Yet sometimes the solutions are simple. I could, of course, take my car to an automatic car wash.

Procrastination is by far the most poisonous and self-defeating behavior we practice. Procrastination literally means betraying our word, thereby diminishing our self-worth. It is in direct opposition to advancement. Procrastination is the most subtle, yet powerful way to draw emotional blood from our prosperity allowance. If we can't trust ourselves, we will not allow advancement. The time to keep our word is not tomorrow; it is now. Keeping our word keeps us moving forward.

Our Heart Is Sacred

All that we do reveals who we are and the perspectives we hold. In my home, there are certain rules. One of them, for example, is that no one enters the house in dirty shoes; this is a rule that is common in many homes. If this is a form of respect for the general living area, what kind of reverence do I have for my most sacred space—the bedroom, the room where we devote six to eight hours of our day to rest, read, and make love?

What is your bedroom like? What does it say about your emotional being? Do you think that the ambience of your bedroom has an effect on your being?

My bedroom is a sanctuary. It is holy. There is no electrical or electronic equipment in it aside from lighting. No TV. It is tidy and orderly. The only thing I do in the bedroom is *converse, read, rest, or make love.*

People who live together sometimes need to discuss matters and occasionally this leads to something complex being discussed directly before they go to sleep. In my home, there is a simple rule that we adhere to: we go to the kitchen or the living room if we have challenging matters to discuss. If we have a difference of opinion, experience resistance to each other's ideas, if we want to discuss something that requires resolution, then we remove ourselves from the sanctity of our bedroom and converse somewhere else.

Our bedroom is a place of peace and refuge that we have always respected. It is truly the heart of my home.

We cannot tramp into the heart's sanctum in dirty shoes with discord on our lips—we have to show it the respect it deserves. Advancement is a sacred process because it is based on the permission or allowance allocated by the heart. This type of advancement is an expression of respect, reverence, and grace, and only by living from the heart can we enjoy the journey, savor the moment, and be in harmony with all.

The analogy serves me well because the bedroom is my sanctuary much like my heart is my base of unity and sincerity. It is the place where I rest, metabolize, rejuvenate, and thereby nurture my advancement.

An Arena of Harmony

As you now understand, we constantly communicate to the world what our intentions are and how worthy of prosperity we feel. The world is communication, the transmission of energy, and the transformation of one type of energy into another in a continual flow. The expression and manifestation of energy materializes the thoughts of every living being in the universe at the frequency or emotional resonance transmitted. The nature of the world is communication and expression. The world is attentive to those who listen to their hearts and allow them to convey the message of their worthiness. The world listens to those who allow their hearts to pulsate at maximum frequency. It is our responsibility to educate the world by conveying to it how to behave toward us and how to support our intentions and our will. It's our responsibility to be as clear, direct, and decisive as possible so that the universal energy can best support our command.

The world provides an arena for harmony for all its beings. When the heart is repressed, shielded, or armored—when its voice is distorted with remorse and regret—the world *still* provides harmony for that voice. In other words, if I communicate to the world that I am undeserving, the world tunes in to that expression, harmonizes with my self-assessment, and sends me people and situations that confirm my self-appraisal. Whether we argue for our greatness or for our limitations, the world endorses our conclusions.

Do you know what has proved to be one of the greatest causes of misfortune? It is to attract wealth, energy, or opportunities that we do not feel worthy of or capable of handling. An example of this is to enjoy a substantial windfall such as winning a lottery. You might think this would be a stroke of fortune. Lots of people dream of suddenly becoming rich. We send wishes like this out into the world and believe that if they are answered the world will be our oyster. "When I become rich, then. . ." However, when we attract energy from lack or the presumption that we will become good enough "when my ship has come in," we are not attracting from a base of worthiness. Therefore, we are not likely to be able to receive such a windfall without major congestion and even disease.

The truth is that only a handful of individuals who win a lottery enjoy improved quality of life or greater prosperity. Most of them cannot bear the burden that comes with sudden riches. They do not feel worthy of what they have attracted and are indeed not equipped to manage that much energy. They can neither manage nor metabolize it. They experience *confuse-stipation* (mental and physical indigestion). This is because advancement or good fortune is not always contingent on the gifts we receive. The same universal laws always apply: when we ingest energy beyond our capacity, there are going to be blockages.

This is why I say, "Everyone is always right." Each of us confirms our vision of the world with our expressed behavior and attracts what is desired to be in harmony with what we see as our advantages or limitations. Whether we assert prosperity or scarcity, we are right. We either intend consciously or unconsciously. Within, there is always an intention that governs our actions that gets communicated to the world. We are always responsible. Our will is always done, whether we choose to allow advancement and prosperity or choose not to choose and allow *imemine* to remain in charge and sustain the spell, the illusion of scarcity.

A Tree Can't Resist Advancement

Look at a tree. A tree has a clear purpose: to transform energy from the sun, from the water, and from the soil to grow, thrive, produce, and reproduce. As the tree grows, its purpose advances. It transforms more energy and grows lusher and more prosperous.

The same principals apply to us. Virtues are stardust, and values are the soil of purpose. They are the foundation that inspires us and infuses us with the passion that fuels our vision. Our vision, in turn, structures the goals to which we are wholeheartedly committed. Our goals are implemented and actualized moment by moment with a permission-based strategy that is grounded in trustworthiness. This is true advancement. When these principals govern our progress, prosperity is a natural flowing miracle of love.

Can you imagine a tree holding itself back, resisting forward movement? A tree's growth is only stunted when it does not have sufficient nourishment from the environment. Trees do not reject nourishment because they regard themselves as undeserving. They do not seek out poor nourishment that will deplete them. They do not distinguish between their roots, their trunks, their branches, or their leaves. They attend to all their parts with the same meticulousness and care. Trees do not deprive themselves of life through rejection.

We are subject to the same laws as the trees and other forms of non-human life—whether we believe this or not. Although a tree cannot purposefully diminish itself, it can find itself in poor soil and cannot change its circumstances. Its growth will be a reflection of its environment. The difference between a tree and us is that we can relocate ourselves and choose or create a new environment.

Advancing into Wellness and Prosperity

Life is not complicated. We understand it instinctively. Our physical posture reveals everything. Energy cannot be constrained. If it appears to be blocked, it has simply been invested in resistance within certain muscles or other body structures. The energy remains there and services our beliefs, expressing what we have consciously or unconsciously requested.

Close your eyes and clench your fists as tightly as possible, and hold them like that for as long as you can. Feel the tension throughout your hands and arms. Feel how it spreads to your shoulders, neck, spine, and skull. Now, relax and open your hands.

This is the difference between holding on and letting go, resisting and not resisting. When you do this exercise, you can easily understand and feel the difference. This is actually quite simple, although it does not always seem to be such a simple matter to stop resisting and just surrender ourselves to light and freedom. Nevertheless, simply opening our hands and unclenching our hearts will allow us to advance into wellness and prosperity.

To let go of resistance is to let go of darkness, prejudice, stasis, tension, defiance, and self-deprivation. To advance is to flow forward with light, energy, understanding, openness, and happiness. So why do we often choose to live in resistance? We are as we are because we want to be that way. There is no point in denying this. It is obvious we brought ourselves here. When we accept responsibility for where we are and for having willed ourselves to this point and have made a commitment to change in order to carry out our purpose, then we will finally be able to allow ourselves to advance and prosper.

We are all as we are because we want to be that way, whether we want to admit to it or not. We will ourselves there. You have to arrive in the present moment before you can advance—you have to acknowledge your own power and become responsible in order to change. That is the beginning. Your choice. Your will.

I am referring to changing your patterns of behavior—not changing you. You are unique. There is only absence and lack to be found in seeking to be different because that means rejecting who you are. When you are fully present, your behavior will change.

There is no setting back the clock, no undoing the past. But you can alter the way you perceive your journey to this moment. The beginning is now. Unless you want to find another set of distractions or illusions that will make you stop, sit down, give up, find some ruse, some angle, some way of setting up a new barrier around the heart. Answer the following questions in your notebook or journal: Are you ready to start the journey now—to allow advancement and prosperity? And to love yourself anyway with all your heart? If not, what is in your way?

Cause and Effect

Energy does not discriminate. It cannot be wasted—only devoted, invested, or allocated to a cause or project. It can never be blocked—only devoted or constrained, consciously or not. Money cannot be spent. It can only be invested in prosperity or scarcity. There is no wrong or right where energy is concerned; there are only consequences. There are no fattening foods only fattening people. These statements may be annoying or even feel hurtful, but they are the premise of responsible advancement. Cause and effect is a universal law that requires acknowledgment if and when you intend to truly advance.

- **There is no such thing as eating too much**—*merely as much as it takes for you to maintain your discomfort and continue self-blame. You're what's eating you!*
- **No one just gets bored**—*if you are bored, it is because you have systematically tired yourself out and practiced various forms of neglect. You bore yourself!*
- **Lateness is intentional**—*we might not admit it, but being late is a choice we make to cause disturbance and resistance within others or ourselves.*

There is no escape from cause and effect. Blinding yourself to this fact means that you are continuing to nourish the *imemine*. You cannot *spend* money. Even if you burn the note we call money, you're only transforming the energy of the paper and thereby creating heat and smoke as you release the energy bound by the paper. The actual funds represented by that note still remain intact in a bank or some other form of deposit. You can only invest it in absence or prosperity. When you accumulate money with fear or lack, the result will only be more fear and lack. When you attract from scarcity, then scarcity is what you attract because the when-disease is what motivates your behavior, not your inspired purpose. Prosperity is the frequency of the heart, a unified field of love. It is not a fragmented energy of duality and lack.

Allowing for Advancement

The first forward movement in prosperity consciousness is to remove our reasons for rejecting and punishing ourselves by letting go of regret and remorse, by forgiving and loving ourselves anyway. Without that, any intentions for change will only breed further absence, and there will be no forward movement. The only way to change what we do is to change how we feel about ourselves and therefore the self-image we project.

To advance, we create a temporary framework or plan for prosperity to dispense with old behavior patterns by being responsible in the present, which gives us the power to replace compulsive behaviors by making choices that allow us to govern our own lives. After that, there is only prosperity and gifts, nothing other than blessings and opportunities.

We practice and train ourselves by implementing new thinking and new behaviors and by solely devoting our awareness to what we do want until we are independent of the constraints and limitations reenacted habitually with impulsive, reactive behaviors dictated by the *imemine*. We trust that things will change, just like a baby learning to speak. They begin by babbling, then they practice and practice until they are finally able to form words.

The framework redirects our attention away from what is habitual and scarcity-driven toward the creative and the positive. It is a process of rebuilding and developing compassionate constructive behavior. The type of framework depends on each individual. We have to design and build it according to our intentions and purpose.

The framework is about confirming our will and strengthening the assertion that we want something other than we have had so far—to show our environment and ourselves that there is some purpose behind our plans and other declared intentions. We confirm for ourselves in our hearts that we are committed. It is essential to change our behavior patterns, to confirm the intent, and to honor our word in order to reaffirm and strengthen our resolve for prosperity.

Our individual journeys are different, and no two people are alike. We create an environment for ourselves where our intentions are supported until we are strong enough to stand on our own two feet. Once you identify what it is you want and muster the courage to declare and commit to your intentions, you're halfway there. Now it's time to affirm your intentions by the framework and structure required to sustain your resolve.

When I make changes in my life, I always begin by writing my intentions in my journal. I edit it until I feel that my mission statement is clear. I identify all the things that are in the way or do not support my intention. I do this by taking a single sheet of paper and drawing a line from top to bottom of the sheet. On the first half, I list the deterrents—whatever is in the way of succeeding. On the other half, I list the supporting elements and what's required to support success. Then, I fold the sheet in half, making sure that the positives are on top so that my awareness is on what I am going to do, not on what I am not going to do. Making this list gives me great clarity. I then use the information to create a structure to support the journey.

The following suggestions will help you promote order and balance:

- Clean up the chaos. Identify charged relationships and resolve them; clean and organize your home and work space; stop making promises you don't intend to keep; and organize your surrounding environment. Scarcity leads to chaos, and chaos leads to scarcity.
- Write down your plans. This significantly multiplies the possibility of success.
- Nourish yourself intentionally and consciously and always with compassion.
- Exercise your body for the sake of well-being and pleasure. This is achieved by respecting your body as the vehicle of your soul and understanding that nurturing them is essential.
- Bring your finances into order by defining how you want to invest your income, energy, and time.
- Keep company with those who support your will to prosper; minimize interactivity with discouraging voices and negative or pessimistic victimizing attitudes.
- Find an advisor or mentor, someone who understands and can listen without bias or codependence.
- Continually practice forgiveness. (The garbage has to be taken out several times a week, not just once.)
- Affirm your intentions by affirming your will to be present so that your heart may be heard as you command your destiny.

Use the above list as ideas or building blocks for the framework you intend to create to support and maximize your advancement and prosperity.

Your Response Is All That Matters

Advancement is contingent upon expressing to the world what it is that we truly desire. We lead by example and by being the change. Suffering is a common form of negative expression. Creativity is the expression of abundance. Advancement is about sharing, expression, and creation—not just communicating, but maximizing and sharing ourselves.

Suffering reveals negativity and lack. All reluctance is a lack of flow, a lack of communication between people, a shortage of positive energy exchange. Reluctance means contraction, rejection, resistance—and the absence of love. People tend to think of advancement or progress in terms of the material world. But there is no difference between the material world and the spiritual world. Everything obeys the same laws; everything reveals its worthiness.

The only thing that matters is what we do with what happens. Our response matters—whether we choose an appropriate response or simply react with a twitch or a reflex and allow the *imemine* to rule. Our response determines whether we advance toward prosperity or remain in scarcity. Our response reveals the level of permission we give ourselves—whether we kick ourselves when we are down or help ourselves to our feet compassionately, whether we love ourselves anyway, and whether we are willing to forgive ourselves.

The challenges we create or attract into our lives and how we resolve them define us—and we all seem to require formidable challenges to awaken from the spell of the *imemine*. Major life challenges cut deep into our emotional lives, but they also provide opportunities for growth or depletion. Death, accidents, and divorce are common types of crises. Let's take a look at the last of these: Divorce is one of the most intense experiences we can encounter. While it can be life-shattering, it can also signal an opportunity for growth. Every loss offers a new path to awakening. Separation with the familiar brings anxiety, but it also brings independence and a heightened understanding of self. There are constant opportunities in life to awaken to our own creation. The transparency of these opportunities is fully revealed once we are conscious and acknowledge how we unconsciously manipulate the energy to reflect and expose our hidden agendas.

Each time we acknowledge and take responsibility for where we have brought ourselves, we become more empowered and better equipped to truly define what we do want by leveraging these challenging experiences and to discover what we don't want and then reaffirm our intentions and advance accordingly.

Letting Go of What Holds Us Back

There is a parable about two monks who went on a journey. They came to a river with a strong current where they met a young woman who asked whether they could help her to cross the river. The elder of the two monks picked up the woman and carried her on his back to the other side. The younger monk said nothing but was clearly upset.

Toward nightfall, the elder monk said to the younger, "Are you alright, brother? You seem upset about something."

"Why did you carry that woman across the river this morning? You know that monks are not supposed to have any interaction with women," replied the younger.

"Well, it's like this," said the elder. "It's hours since I carried her across the river. But she is clearly still a burden to you."

This parable leads to the question: How do we define interaction? When are we interacting with one another and when not? Are we interacting when we hold a grudge, feel anger, or harbor resentment? At what point do we let go? How long do we want to carry the burden? What do we have invested in regret and remorse? Why do we hold on to grudges? What's the payoff for investing our energy in self-pity or martyrdom? Could it possibly be to avoid advancement and to sustain the pain and discomfort to which we are so emotionally addicted?

When we are truly ready to advance, we forgive all and release the foul-smelling debris from the so-called past. We no longer hold ourselves back or constrain ourselves. We assume the leadership role in our lives, progress, and move forward. In other words, we lift the spell, open our hearts, and embrace the world.

Living Life Fully in Forward Motion

The difference between leaders and micromanagers is trust. The leader knows what he wants to accomplish and consciously devotes the energy with clear purpose and intention to the mission at hand, providing the environment, direction, and trust required to inspire prosperity. Micromanagement means to doubt, and to trust means to strengthen. To live fully means to trust yourself and live from the heart and prosper in the moment. Living life fully means that:

- Our thoughts, words, and behavior are in harmony with our will and purpose.
- We enjoy prosperity.
- We are worthy and deserve to realize our goals.
- We experience our goals in the moment.
- We trust ourselves and believe that we have the ability to confirm our intentions.
- Our self-image is radiant and harmonious.
- We set ourselves challenging and realizable goals.
- We advance toward our goals with an inner purpose, clear intentions, and a vision inspired by love.
- We are determined and tenacious and always realize our goals.
- Our purpose is built on foundation and commitment.
- We have restored trust in ourselves and faith in life.
- We welcome any positive criticism that encourages us to examine and assess our perspectives.
- We are passionate and full of inspiration.
- We are no longer manipulated by the illusions of the *imemine*.

Each moment we breathe, we may choose to be inspired, infused by the divine energy. Each moment we live, we may choose to be enthused with passion and devote our energy and light to transform our lives and our world by being conscious, purposeful, vibrant, and fully alive creators.

Advancement means to fully express the language of our heart's desire, and then project our vision onto the large screen of life and clearly communicate our purpose and commitment to the rest of the world. Advancement means that we no longer hold back or restrain the light. We are fully alive; we are love.

This is how I choose to live my life: aware, responsible, purposeful, committed, and fully alive. I still fall unconscious occasionally, and I love myself anyway. I am still challenged by life, and I am grateful for the lessons. "When you're green, you're growing. When you're ripe, you start to rot." I live by these words and acknowledge that it's my responsibility to generate the interest and purpose to sustain my light, my growth. I love myself!

Measuring Advancement

The measure of advancement is simple: it is the frequency of emotion experienced and expressed in association with our purpose, vision, goals, and level of commitment. Is the emotion we are experiencing in harmony with the rhythm of our heart? Does it resonate with prosperity? The ultimate indicator of our advancement is whether or not we are infused with interest and passion for the task at hand as well as toward life and the purpose we serve. "To dare is to lose your foothold for a moment. To not dare is to lose yourself." This is where our permission is fully revealed. This is true revelation.

To take the step

out
of range of time the sniper

free
from the siege of days that kill

released
from suffocating habit

over
the barbed wire fence of doubt

take a step

backward

to the cloudless space
where all begins anew

—*Ari Jóhannesson*

To Will Is to Act

Advancement is acting from the heart. Our actions reveal our intentions. Take out your journal or notebook. Review and document your current progress. Acknowledge that your resistance to change reveals your attachment to your current situation. Review each of the daily reflection assignments you have completed so far before moving on to the Daily Reflections on the following page.

daily reflections

Ask yourself the following questions and be prepared to record the answers in your notebook or journal. (Your response can be as simple as yes or no. If no, also answer why not. If yes, answer what that means and looks like to you.)

- Am I present and accounted for?

- Have I forgiven myself—am I fully responsible?

- Have I defined my purpose?

- Is my vision vivid and are my goals S.M.A.R.T.?

- Am I fully committed to my life?

- Is my heart open to prosperity and advancement?

- Am I advancing, holding back, or retreating?

- Am I fully engaged in life or despondent?

- How do I reveal my worth?

- Am I straining or forcing my progress?

- Am I fully alive or constrained?

Insight

Witnessing Our Wellness and Prosperity Evolve

"There is a universal, intelligent life force that exists within everyone and everything. It resides within each one of us as a deep wisdom, an inner knowing. We can access this wonderful source of knowledge and wisdom through our intuition, an inner sense that tells us what feels right and true for us at any given moment."

—SHAKTI GAWAIN

Insight

is the permanent state of awareness.
It is the compassionate witness
experiencing the present moment
from the premise of the heart.
There is intimacy, unity
& love in every breath.

Step 6. Insight

Insight is similar to awareness, but it is more objective. It is the ability to be attentive within ourselves while also being in touch with what is outside us. Some call it "witnessing"—not just a single a flash of intuition, but a continuous state of observing life as it unfolds. Others say it is a constant dialogue between the soul and the outside world. Insight is openness and clarity, the ability to see things as they truly are, without prejudice and without resistance. Insight means living from the unity of the heart, not the illusions of the mind, with the awareness necessary to distinguish between them.

We usually think of insight as a single act or moment, a flash of intuition that comes and then goes. However, insight can also be continuous. Here, insight is *inner sight*, a state of observation in which we witness life as it unfolds. It is pure awareness—a constant dialogue between the being within and the outside world, always on the premises of the heart and never on those of the *imemine*. Insight is openness and clarity, the ability to see things as they truly are without prejudice or resistance.

To have insight is to be present and alert, constantly—not to receive an occasional message from the heart but to be constantly in communication with it. While we are insightful, we are close enough to ourselves to hear the frequency at which our heart beats and thereby to experience things as they are.

Those who are available to be a witness in their own existence with full objectivity and compassion will awaken to what some call the gift of grace, an energy or a power that any superhero would be proud of. This kind of individual never makes mistakes. I mean it. This kind of individual sees all of his or her actions as fortunate—especially those actions and deeds that might be categorized as mistakes under ordinary circumstances. The reason is that "mistakes" reveal illusions and are thereby transformed into blessings and excellent opportunities for even further revelations, deepening our self-understanding and further weakening the *imemine*. This individual never kicks himself when he is down because he made a "mistake." Instead, he is grateful for the blessing and the opportunity to learn and mature.

This is the difference between a pro and an amateur. The pro corrects his so-called mistakes with compassion and helps himself back to his feet. The amateur not only kicks himself when he is down, but also uses the fall (which he sees as a result of a mistake he made) to motivate the *imemine* and urge it on to greater deeds.

A great superpower is accessed by simply refraining from self-judgment, when we have gained the insight and ability to support ourselves instead of abandoning, betraying, and rejecting ourselves. When we are presented with an opportunity or a challenge, we can choose to respond, after having contemplated the possibilities with inner light. We have gained an insight into our patterns of behavior and become a conscious observer.

By constantly cultivating awareness, you will become fully *responsible* to forgive yourself in all areas of your life. You reclaim the energy invested in remorse and devote the energy to your purpose, vision, and goals. You are fully committed to advancement and you prosper and thrive as a result. When you are fully present, you become a witness to your own existence and can devote attention to various things, both within you and around you without having to attach any special meaning to them. You become an objective witness—a spectator who enjoys observing what is transpiring in the present moment. Insight is illumination—a dialogue with soul.

Experiencing and Nurturing Grace

Permission becomes revealed through advancement. Through our actions, we reveal to the world how worthy we feel in our hearts, and we ask it to ration out prosperity or scarcity on that basis. Insight allows us to be present to our advancement. In grace, personal authorization reveals the prosperity we are prepared to allow ourselves. When we are insightful, we are passionate about being alive, about breathing, and all our senses become heightened. We dare to turn the corner, trust ourselves and the world, and experience love for all things. When we fall down, we pull ourselves back up to our feet immediately. When we are insightful, we understand the context of cause and effect. We move to a new rhythm, express love in the moment, and take our part in the cosmic dance, constantly advancing.

When we are insightful, we know the potential of our power and how brightly our light shines. We understand that all of us are spiritual beings that have the *imemine* (which obeys the "laws of the jungle") living within us. Instead of rejecting or ignoring this fact, we use our brightest light to expose the *imemine* and thereby render it powerless.

Revealing the Agenda

When we have obtained insight, the nourishment we choose (whatever it may be) is no longer an opportunity for rejection. There is no right or wrong food. Food is energy and a source of replenishment for the mind and the body. How we invest the energy and the quality of the energy is always chosen to sustain prosperity or lack. Some foods are organic and wholesome while other foods are completely nutrient deficient and actually noxious. The difference between the choices we make when we nourish is solely contingent on what we intend to nourish and sustain. Our intentions are either wholesome or unwholesome; food is only a passive tool. We are, however, either an aggressor or a lover. When we are conscious of what we do, lovingly and without pronouncing judgment, there is no longer any sense of transgression or betrayal. The only thing left are the choices we make; only the laws of cause and effect remain. And those who live in light and love are always capable of accepting the consequences of their actions without judging or punishing themselves.

The Best We Can Do

Living life as a witness does not necessarily mean continuous happiness or harmony. Living with insight means living in transparency, truthfully; there are no more hidden agendas. The *imemine* does not expire until the body does. The best we can do is to render it powerless and send it into deep and protracted hibernation. And because the *imemine* will always be a part us, the need for constant awareness will remain. That is what is called insight—to be aware in awareness. To love yourself enough to be aware all the time; to love yourself enough to catch yourself red-handed without accusation or punishment . . . and still love yourself; to love yourself enough to create a framework built on your vision, purpose, goals, and love; to be aware and to direct your awareness into being sure that your behavior correlates with your framework and your declared intentions.

A Personal Story of Recognizing Self-Rejection

The *imemine*, like any parasite, cannot survive without its host and will always be ready to shift its location in an effort to survive. Here is an example: A short while ago, I had a sudden bout of what turned out to be lumbago, although at the time it felt more like a slipped disc. I was unfit for work for the best part of a week. The pain ran down my back, through my buttocks, along the entire length of my right leg, and into my toes. I placed myself in the hands of some people I trusted to facilitate the process of healing without my being judgmental about or afraid of the discomfort I was experiencing. They employed massage therapy, flower essences, and various methods of healing. With the help of these good people, I discovered that this lumbago was connected to at least three areas of my life.

First, it was connected to the death of my father and our joint history, which of course is not over even though he has passed. Fortunately, I am still here to metabolize the energy that was once my father. Second, I have simply not allowed myself time in the past year to listen to the messages that pointed to what was happening in my back. Now, I finally had time to wind down, stay home, breathe slowly, and take a look into my behavior patterns of defiance and insecurity.

Third, my company was beginning to grow and expand, which triggered certain patterns of control and permission inside me, bringing to the surface some of my insecurities regarding expansion and the challenges of delegation. In other words, I was *holding back* and restricting my advancement.

I suspected that these three things lay behind my lumbago, but that isn't the point of the story. After a few days in the care of these good friends and some days of rest at home, although not having fully recovered in my back and my legs, the discomfort was gradually subsiding. I had just completed a session at my physiotherapist when I had the insight to see how the *imemine* had snuck in. I caught myself thinking, *My word, I can't wait until I've fixed this . . .*

So, what's wrong with thinking that, you might ask? My answer is that I was rejecting myself *in the moment*. It is the same thing as saying to myself, *I am not good enough. I don't want to be like this now. I want to be different.* And that is a vote of no confidence, a rejection of the present, a rejection of myself. The *imemine* was rejecting me, but my heart responded quickly and whispered, *Trust me.*

As soon as I understood the illusion of doubt that had so subtly undermined me, I felt my whole body relax and a wave of confidence ran through me. That was when the healing began—when I sent my body a message that I trusted it to be as it was and facilitate its own healing. The resistance disappeared, the flow began, and my heart regained the space to pulsate at full strength and allow the light to shine freely.

Self-rejection is only brought about by a figment of the mind—it can never take place where there is love or light. It is a cruel game played by the *imemine*. When a part of your life expresses itself—for example, in a sore throat, aches or pains, or an impending illness—we should welcome that expression and not resist. The disease only begins when we feel sorry for ourselves and reject discomfort, when we actually proclaim ourselves to be sick. It is at this moment we cease to be strong. *Absence is the mother of all disease.*

Being a Compassionate Witness

Insight is an objective position. It is the observation of a witness who is closely aware of what he or she sees. A witness only conveys information. A witness does not judge. A witness is present and simply conveys what has been observed.

What does it mean when I encourage you to be insightful, to be a witness in your life without attaching or fettering your perception to any given meaning, good or bad? As a witness, you objectively observe without judging or predicting unpleasant consequences either for yourself or for others. This means there are various roles (which you may be very used to playing) that you *cannot* assume at the same time: *gossip, the neighborhood watch, the cop, the district attorney, the judge, the prison guard,* or *the executioner.* When you are a compassionate witness, you cannot attend to any of these roles.

The most challenging thing about *not* living as a witness is not living with insight. In that case, you are judge, jury, and executioner in your own life. So, are you guilty? You may say, "Yes, no doubt about it. I have been watching myself for some time and the evidence is overwhelming. I am as guilty as sin." If that is what you believe, answer these questions: How long is your sentence? How severe is your punishment? How long a spell in prison are you talking about here? What about parole? Would you consider a suspended sentence? Are you permitted visits from your family, friends, or maybe your heart on the weekends? Or are you in solitary confinement? Who has the authority to make these decisions?

When we decide how long our sentence is, we can begin looking at ways to improve or reform ourselves. But instead, we often choose to keep ourselves in straightjackets for indefinite periods of time and for undefined crimes with no possibility of parole—and on charges that we would never level at anyone else. We choose to leverage blame to sustain our victimhood. When we are ready to prosper, we choose to forgive ourselves and to love and advance prosperity. Awareness is the key to liberty and transformation. Insight is the tool required to sustain awareness, to be in a constant state of witnessing. Insight means observing from the heart, being a leader. It means being responsible, purposeful, committed, and mindfully progressive. This is being a conscious creator. Insight is the vehicle to nurture and sustain that liberty, free will, purpose, commitment, and prosperity.

Here I Am, Present and Insightful

Here I am—in contact and communication with my heart. I am aware and in harmony with my surroundings, my inside world, the outside world, the universe. It is with reason that I speak of the tune of the heart because all the words used in this dialogue, both in English and in older languages such as Greek and Latin, suggest musical harmony. Concord means "hearts together," in harmony; the word "universe" is a combination of "one" and "verse"—a shared song. *Insight, intimacy, intuitive*—all of these words reveal a harmonious heart pulsing and transmitting in unity with all resonating hearts—"one-verse"; one universe.

To Be a Witness

You're out driving. Conditions have been good, but the weather changes just as you turn off the highway. It begins to grow dark, and it starts to rain. You turn on your headlights, tighten your grip on the wheel, and devote all your attention to the task at hand.

You do not blame the weather or the darkness. Nor do you blame the rain or the road. You consider the conditions in which you find yourself, and then do your best to make your way through the situation as calmly as possible and without being affected by distractions.

In short, you do not resist a situation over which you have no control. Instead of being distracted, you become fully present—and therefore in the position of a witness who observes all that is going on without emotional attachment. You understand that at any given moment you can be present to the journey or be absent and risk running your car into a ditch. The same is true for life.

Attending to Intimacy

Intimacy, integrity, and generosity are the prerequisites of prosperity and are synonymous with being present, sincerely available, loving, and caring. Being present is therefore synonymous with insight—everything being evident, transparent, and pure in the now. Absolute honesty and trust equals generosity and abundance. Prosperity means to be intimate and fully available each moment, to thrive, to be fully alive, and to be love.

Intimacy is a significant consequence of the first five steps—personal intimacy, to be intimate with your qualities and your resistance toward your full expression, to be lovingly intimate with the present moment and the actuality of your creation.

The mark of a good emotional relationship is feeling intimate, and your heart knows exactly what I mean. Absence has been more or less our dominant state, willing or unwilling, by default. Love is our natural state, and absence is an illusion. As soon as we stop attending to intimacy, we are attending to absence by default and therefore heading toward separation and pain.

When you are not attending to intimacy, you are attending to the opposite: separation. This analogy applies to all areas of our lives. Remember, all that you devote your attention to grows and thrives. What you are cultivating does not just thrive on its own. If you live with someone, the relationship requires attention for it to be loving and intimate. This might consist in small details and actions, but most of all, it is about awareness and attention—about being attentive to your partner, about letting him or her feel how much you value and respect them and thereby strengthening your union.

When you do not do this and devote little interest in a relationship—when you are not attentive and do not engage your partner's deepest feelings—it is the same as not watering or nourishing a plant. It grows pale, withers, and dies.

Doing nothing is in itself a course of action, just as not making a choice is a choice not to choose. If we want the grass to grow and the flowers to blossom we have to water them. If we do not water them, we are deciding to let them wither and die. When we nourish our relationship with ourselves, it grows. When we do not nourish it, we invite detachment and fragmentation, the opposite of unity. There is no insight, presence, or unity without intimacy.

"Intimacy" is sometimes translated as "into me you see" and with some justification. Intimacy means being so close to someone else that they can see into you—literally perceive your innermost core. It also means being so close to yourself that you can see your own innermost core, literally touch your own heart, to be touched, in grace. We can never show anyone more than we have revealed to ourselves. We cannot lead others to a place we have not dared to go ourselves. When we are insightful, we are revealing ourselves. We dare to be open and vulnerable because we trust our hearts.

That is why we choose to be present and therefore insightful. We want to be so close to ourselves that we feel the full gravity of our own presence. We want to trust ourselves to bear scrutiny and to be so present and in touch that we can fully understand what we are experiencing each moment—whether it is a beautiful moment with a loved one or a challenging confrontation.

In all circumstances, it is possible to ask yourself the following questions: Am I intimate with my own existence, with the circumstances and emotions they awaken in me, right now? Am I a compassionate witness with respect to the situation I am in or am I a biased judge who sees only lack and suffering, looking for a good story to fill up the emptiness—for example, *This is happening because . . . This would never have happened if it hadn't been for . . .* Or do I see my circumstances as a challenging gift, a blessing that reveals me in this moment—an opportunity to tailor my advancement accordingly?

Forced Intimacy or Presence

To have insight is to be present and accounted for. There are several ways to bring about forced or exaggerated presence in which a person experiences a heightened sense of life. For example, most of us have felt the exhilaration of a new relationship where romance and excitement are at a peak and the body becomes so sensitized that every cell is eager to engage. Similarly, the adrenaline rush we experience when confronting a life-threatening situation is particularly intense. Indeed, it can be so exhilarating that some people are constantly putting themselves in harm's way by engaging in various high-risk activities. Anyone who practices a dangerous sport needs to be 100 percent present, totally aware with their entire body and soul alert just to survive the moment. I call this forced intimacy or presence. This is not to belittle the experience, but rather to point out that it is not permanent and therefore just as much of a distraction as any other addiction.

Intimacy or presence in extreme situations is attractive and enticing, but it is based on a need to thrust ourselves into certain situations to feel fully alive. One form of this need for forced presence is when we go into the safe and secure environment of a cinema to watch a horror movie—beside ourselves with fear may be the closest we can get to real intimacy.

Presence is power. To be intimate is to be unified and accounted for. The previous five steps illustrate that without being aware, responsible, purposeful, and committed, we will not allow or permit intimacy. Remember, you are the power and the glory. To will is to act. Lovingly and tenderly choose to show up in your own life and intimately experience the present *you*. Allow love.

Energy Tells the Truth

Every second is an opportunity with two alternatives: we can react and become absent and reject this opportunity in a flash in a multitude of ways *or* we can respond and be a witness and observe in the light of compassion. It is not possible to do both. Just as light excludes the dark, one excludes the other. Insight makes it possible for a person to know exactly and instantly which way has been chosen. How? Because the light will dim as soon as absence, resistance, or rejection is enacted. Energy always tells its own story about whether we are here or have left. We immediately sense our weakness and are not completely ourselves. Absence is dark and lonely, and we always feel the constraint of absence. We *always* know when the light diminishes.

A plan of action has to be formulated immediately. Insight is attention coupled with the will to act—with insight you can see with the eyes of the soul. It is always a flash, not a thought, just pure observation and attention, awareness, clarity. If attachments or doubts surface, they are reflected by the duality of mind, the *imemine,* not from the unity of heart. Each moment in insight represents new beginnings, an opportunity to see things as they truly are and elect to change course, if necessary, and embark upon a journey of true prosperity, insightfulness, and to live fully alive.

The Heart's Foremost Function Is to Sense

Insight is pure awareness; it is when the heart is directly connected. When you are truly intimate with yourself, you experience the frequency of the heart as a light tremble that ripples through all the cells of your body like a light breeze. Sensing and understanding always follows this pattern: the heart senses something; it is aware of energy and frequency. Then our sense-perception system takes in information via sight, taste, hearing, and touch. The heart sends this to the brain and the brain distributes that information to the relevant parts of the body. With insight, we can leverage this information by being in tune with the heart and then ground, synchronize, and unify the activity of our brain, mind, and heart.

"Waiting" for the Green Man

A few years ago, I decided to obey all traffic regulations. I was tired of always exceeding the speed limit by a few miles per hour—especially since I rarely had good reason to hurry. During this switch, one of the things I found most challenging was obeying the traffic signals for pedestrians.

The "green man light" tells us when it is safe to cross; the "red man light" tells us not to cross. I did not like having to stop walking when I saw the "red man" light, finding it a waste of time to wait for the green one. I had come to see this signal as one of the least important of all traffic rules—the kind I had no need to follow.

However, I decided to make the traffic lights my beacon of presence—a tool to practice being in the moment and not to resist the natural flow of life, even though that flow was designed by man. I realized how much it simplified matters and conserved my energy. I no longer had to preoccupy myself and assess the situation at a crossing, and I learned the difference between *waiting* and *being*.

I stopped *waiting* for the green man, and instead, inhabited the present moment by being insightful and observant instead of defiant, agitated, and absent. Then life appeared right in front of my face; everything became vivid and my senses heightened. I was present in my life by choice.

Not Me—Just Us

Whoever understands that there is no me—just us—touches God. They understand that energy is endless and boundless. It starts nowhere and ends nowhere. It just is—always. Those who understand this love all that is. The following quote by Marianne Williamson illustrates the opportunity that we have been blessed to be presented with. Our personal perspectives reflect our prosperity permission. The constraints or the resistance we experience always reveals our true potential as the light proceeds to shine through the illusion and liberate us from our spell. Insight reveals your unlimited potential as it urges you to let go of the emotional constraints and enter the light and be love.

"Our deepest fear is not that we are inadequate. Our deepest fear is that we are powerful beyond measure. It is our light, not our darkness that most frightens us. We ask ourselves, Who am I to be brilliant, gorgeous, talented, fabulous? Actually, who are you not to be? You are a child of God. Your playing small does not serve the world. There is nothing enlightened about shrinking so that other people won't feel insecure around you. We are all meant to shine, as children do. We were born to make manifest the glory of God that is within us. It's not just in some of us; it's in everyone. And as we let our own light shine, we unconsciously give other people permission to do the same. As we are liberated from our own fear, our presence automatically liberates others."

—Marianne Williamson

Flowers always open as they should, as if that was always the plan. With insight, the heart attends to how you blossom. It sees clearly and makes no judgment on your advancement. With insight, the heart is full of passion. It adores what happens, and you enjoy being a miracle. All is revealed.

daily reflections

Ask yourself the following questions and be prepared to record the answers in your notebook or journal. (Your response can be as simple as yes or no. If no, also answer why not. If yes, answer what that means and looks like to you.)

• Am I intimate?

• Do I practice being present?

• Am I observing advancement from my heart?

• Am I "in sight"?

• Am I intuitive?

• Am I the blessing or the curse in my life?

• Do I kick myself when I am down or help myself back to my feet?

• Am I an amateur or a professional?

• Do I love myself anyway?

Gratitude

Counting Our Blessings

"We can set our deeds to the music of a grateful heart, and seek to round our lives into a hymn—the melody of which will be recognized by all who come in contact with us, and the power of which shall not be evanescent, like the voice of the singer, but perennial, like the music of the spheres."

—WILLIAM MACKERGO TAYLOR

Gratitude

is enlightenment. It is the glow of generosity expressed by blessing each moment. It is the realization that awareness is the primary asset and that when you love fully, you are complete and prosperous: You are enlightened.

Step 7. Gratitude

Gratitude is what we accept from the world with grace. It is seeing life as a series of challenges and opportunities, not as a series of rejections. Gratitude nourishes the heart and is liberation from habit, absence, addiction, and desire. It is a response to the generosity of the universe. Gratitude is not a prayer for something that is lacking, a cure for a specific ill, or blind hope. Rather it is an exultation, a release from the bonds of negation, appreciation for our blessings. It is the reallocation of energy. Gratitude is enlightenment. Gratitude is the power of presence—true ever-lasting prosperity, moment by moment.

Gratitude is enlightenment. When we are sincerely grateful, we experience a deep feeling of worthiness and prosperity. We can feel our own being. We can feel *us* in our souls. We can feel everything and everyone that is. We can feel God.

In gratitude nothing is lacking. There is just us and the world—complete, in the now. That is how artists, leaders, and creators manifest themselves—in the present with complete freedom. This step is not about *thinking about* gratitude or saying, *"I am grateful."* Rather, it is the *feeling and experience of* gratitude. When this takes place, we are in the present moment, and we truly experience prosperity and feel the pulsing of our hearts. When we feel gratitude, there is no room for anything else—no lack, no anxiety, no self-pity. Our beings are filled with gratitude. We are inspired by gratitude, enlightened.

I am not using the word "enlightened" in the sense that one is wise, but rather I am using it to mean that when we are enlightened, we are brimming with light, the sacred light of the present, the love that fills the world. Gratitude is light—which means that darkness is just the absence of gratitude; it is ingratitude. Truth is always light; all else is illusion.

The opposite of gratitude is rejection, resistance, self-pity, and abandonment. In modern society, we devote a great deal of energy in intending to be happy—and we are happy, intermittently, usually when we have achieved a particular goal.

What we often see as irritations, inconveniences, and disturbances are actually the gifts of life: clues, indications, and opportunities. Somehow, we miss the essence that is presented to us when we collide with other energies, what we sometimes call *misfortune* or *accident*. We forget that the greatest opportunities reside in everyday events rather than in major occurrences. We have a tendency to make little of the gifts of life and absolutely nothing out of our misfortunes. Our greatest opportunities lie in the events that reveal us to ourselves and which prompt us to awaken.

Ingratitude is the absence of light; anxiety. Gratitude is light, peace; it is love.

What Is Gratitude?

What are the conditions required to be grateful? How do we experience and demonstrate gratitude? Does gratitude come from an obligation to reciprocate? Is it merely a gesture, a learned response, a courtesy? Gratitude is so much more than any of these. Gratitude is choosing to see life as a blessing—when you count your blessings and give thanks for the experience that adversity brings you. Gratitude comes about the instant you allow things to be as they are, when you embrace the moment, when you *feel* to your heart's capacity. Those who are not living from the sincerity of the heart can never *experience* gratitude. They can think about it, talk about it, and be polite; they can even show a certain kindness in what they say and do, but they cannot experience gratitude before they embrace things as they are.

Gratitude is peace of heart and mind: gratitude is nourishing the vehicle of our soul lovingly, and intentionally; it is trusting the unfolding of life in love, a sensation of inner warmth. Gratitude is the satisfaction, happiness, joy, and bliss we experience as we celebrate life moment by moment. It is the warm fuzzy feeling of ecstasy that emanates from the heart.

How do we recognize enlightened beings? Do they look saintly or emanate holiness? Not necessarily. Often, they are recognizable because they do not take themselves seriously. They live in the present with perpetual gratitude and respond to life moment by moment from insight; they do not react impulsively. They are liberated from entertaining the *imemine*. They are free of the oppression of having to fit in with their surroundings. They are not dependent on any general rules or assumptions or what the rest of us perceive as reality. Enlightened beings have arrived at an at-one-ness where they experience their environment as a constant miracle, a continuous, harmonious universe. They perceive that all is complete. Enlightened beings do not resist life and their hearts pulse and emanate power and light. There are many enlightened beings among us. However, they are only evident to other enlightened beings. Just as we can only give what we have, we can only relate on our level of vibration. Aspire to be enlightened by being grateful, by counting your blessings, and by being love, and then the enlightened ones will appear.

> The others are we.
> We are one.
> We are everything.
> All is one.
> All is love.

This is what enlightened beings sense and understand. This is inherent in all of us.

We are complete and fully nourished by gratitude in the present; we are brimming with life. Einstein captures the essence of enlightenment in the following quote by encouraging us to open our heart, to embrace all of life as one, and thus lift the spell by entering the light.

"A human being is a part of a whole, called by us universe, a part limited in time and space. He experiences himself, his thoughts and feelings as something separated from the rest . . . a kind of optical delusion of his consciousness. This delusion is a kind of prison for us, restricting us to our personal desires and to affection for a few persons nearest to us. Our task must be to free ourselves from this prison by widening our circle of compassion to embrace all living creatures and the whole of nature in its beauty."

—Albert Einstein

Gratitude is unity, a sense of oneness, a powerful and palpable feeling of belonging in the universe, a feeling of being at home with all of creation. Gratitude is also understanding in our hearts and throughout the cells of our bodies that rejection is simply resistance against the present moment. Most of us experience rejection as being deeply personal. We feel that others are rejecting us. But that is simply not possible. Rejection lies entirely within us—nowhere other than in our own reactions and attitudes toward our own self-image. Rejection cannot be personal. Other people cannot reject us because the experience is ours alone.

Along these lines, you can never be angry with anyone other than yourself. The people you choose to be angry with are only substitutes who serve to maintain illusion and defensiveness, substitutes that you need to use because the *imemine* always wants to be a victim and never demonstrate anger against itself. You are always responsible for your own feelings.

If you do not reject yourself, no one else can reject you. If you are grateful for each passing moment without judging it, you will never experience rejection.

"Did you change your mind about dying?"

I went to my foster-sister Jónína's home to celebrate what would have been my father's seventy-fifth birthday. When I reached her front door, a five-year-old urchin stood and asked me straight out, "Did you change your mind about dying?"

I answered, "Yes, I'm going to live!"

"So, you got better then?" she asked me searchingly.

"Yes, I'm well," I said and then she let me in.

This five-year-old had gone to the hospital with her parents to see my father. She had been told he was dying. When she saw me, she mistook me for him. She thought I was my father, Gunnar, risen from the dead. It seemed entirely reasonable to her. And she was partly right: I am my father.

What I experienced when my father passed was gratitude and grace. My father lives on in me, that part of my father that I cultivate and devote attention to. I was fortunate enough to enjoy a close relationship with him, even though there was often a great physical distance between us. I have not sensed any change in that relationship since he passed.

This opportunity has encouraged me to look at my past in the context of that defining moment, and it reminds me of the time my father and I went to the Kripalu Center for Yoga & Health in Massachusetts about thirty years ago. Before we attended the ten-day workshop "The Advanced Self," we were instructed to bring some personal possession from our childhood, something we connected with emotionally or of which we were especially fond.

At a certain moment in the workshop, all those attending (about thirty in total) were asked to sit a circle and put whatever they had brought inside that circle. This was a ceremony to help us all dispense with regret and remorse and enjoy a sense of freedom from our perceived past.

When it came to me, I calmly approached my father, bent down, placed my hands under his legs and back, picked him up, and placed him inside the circle. There were bursts of laughter and everyone clearly enjoyed this, but I was absolutely serious. I was fortunate enough to be already free of the past that the facilitators wanted to liberate me from.

I was grateful for my father and that was exactly what I wanted to contribute to the course. I wanted to show the effect he had on my life. This gesture also had quite an effect on the workshop itself, and everyone understood the relationship between myself and my father was peaceful and unique.

My father will never cease to live. We all return to Mother Earth as he has done, but something of him lives on in me. I feel a deep sense of awe and admiration when I think of him, and since he passed I continue to celebrate his life instead of grieving his death.

My father is within me and his essence is a part of me. I am also my mother. I am my parents—and one of the greatest rejections we experience is to be contemptuous or condescending of our parents because it means we despise ourselves. If you have unresolved emotional issues attached to your parents, you possess a huge energetic recovery opportunity. There is a saying I heard many years ago that sounds something like this: "If you think you're enlightened, go visit with your parents for a couple of days." The intent of the saying is to illustrate that most people have unresolved issues with their parents, and even though they may be passive at a distance, they will flare up in their presence. At any time we may choose to become adults by forgiving ourselves and become responsible for how we feel and where we have brought ourselves. The instance we truly do, we recover the power we have invested in blame and victimhood.

Assume your power and devote your awareness to the quality and beauty within your parents, the same quality and beauty that's within you. Acknowledge that we have all contributed to the journey and that by changing our perspective and the role we have chosen to play everything changes and becomes a blessing. Gratitude is grace; when we express gratitude, we become a blessing, a miracle.

I have never experienced losing my father because I am my father, and I am grateful for the opportunity to continue to work with the energy that was him. Alive or deceased, our parents are the most powerful reflectors of how we truly feel about ourselves. Their role or service is eternal, the bond is eternal, and we alone can change the energetic structure or the service we subscribe to. The moment you love yourself, you love your parents. The moment you are grateful, you become a blessing to all. Let go and be. Let go and love.

Counting Our Blessings

The power of awareness and faith has so often been confirmed. Recently, the Psychology Department of the University of Harvard carried out a study on a group of eighty-four women, all of whom did physically demanding work as hotel maids. According to a questionnaire completed before the study, none of the women considered that they did any kind of planned exercise or physical fitness.

The women were then divided into two groups. The first group was given a detailed account of what physical effects their work was having on them—what each part of their jobs did for specific muscles and how many calories they burned. The women were informed that the physical movement they carried out at work was sufficient to meet the recommendations of the Surgeon General on an active and healthy life. While the study was being carried out, this information was made constantly and visibly available so that all the women could see the results.

Meanwhile the control group received no information at all.

At the end of the study, it turned out that the first group had achieved greater physical health (based on weight, body-fat percentage, fat-to-muscle ratio, vital statistics, and blood pressure). The only difference between them and the control group was that they were constantly aware of the physical benefits of their daily work. They did not experience their work as being difficult but as a series of opportunities that were physically beneficial. In other words, they counted their blessings, not their curses.

Close your eyes and think about a normal day in your life. Are you counting your blessings or your curses? For most of us, a bad memory is more tangible than a good one, a negative emotion is more familiar than a positive one. That is why most people I have encountered are more preoccupied with counting their curses than their blessings. They shine the powerful light of attention on their curses, and they become more obtrusive with every passing day, predictably enough because of the devotion bestowed upon them.

When I start the day with the thought that I am going to experience prosperity, love, and satisfaction, for example by looking at my wife, my children, and my family, and seeing what I have to be grateful for, I know that the opposite would be true if I devoted the same amount of attention to what I lack.

Everything to which we devote our attention grows and flourishes. We know that whether we devote our attention to something we want or do not want, it still flourishes to the same extent. The will directs our attention and shines a light on what it wants. The key here is to decide to devote our awareness to gratitude and to nourish it and cultivate it like a flower so that it will flourish, grow, and be fragrant. There is no positive or constructive payoff if we devote our attention to weeds and absence.

Gratitude is a choice we make. It means to be in a state of gratitude and to count our blessings rather than our curses. If we do that, our blessings will increase and our negative constraints will decrease. One way we can exercise gratitude is by writing down all that we are grateful for. Gradually, the scope of our gratitude will increase. When we connect with our gratitude emotionally, it obtains power.

When we reach Step 7 by moving through each of the earlier steps, we will have adopted an attitude of gratitude we give thanks for everything there is a reason to be thankful for—for our blessings and all that we sense is good in our lives. We give thanks again and again for these things. Then, after a certain amount of time, we can choose to give thanks for something else: we can choose to give thanks for our "curses" or afflictions—for things we have considered as negative in our lives. That is when we arrive at a place where everything has a right to exist, a place where there is no longer any need for judgment, a place where all is blessed, a place where all is as it should be. In this place, blessings and curses become indistinguishable, where they merge into one great blinding light.

A place where all is blessed.

A place where we are enlightened.

When Will Your Moment Arrive?

At what stage in your life are you going to come to fruition? After which achievement? After how many yoga classes? After what number of self-help books? After accruing how many millions of dollars? How many university diplomas or degrees? How many children or grandchildren? When is the right time? When will you allow yourself to say *now*?

When we finally want and choose to be responsible for purpose in our own lives . . . when we choose to trust and bless . . . when we cherish purpose and have clear intention . . . when we no longer "wish and hope and think and pray," as the song goes . . . when we no longer bemoan our misfortune, concentrating on our disappointments in darkness and ingratitude, because it doesn't serve us anymore . . . when all of our energy is invested by conscious choice in prosperity . . . when we have relinquished the "curse" and adopted the light, the "blessings" . . . when we acknowledge that our perspectives determine our experiences and that we are the creator of our lives, the masters of our destiny. That's when our moment has arrived.

Many people understand this well, but still resist blossoming because they do not allow themselves to feel worthy, yet. They still convince themselves that they will not live up to their expectations. They are frightened of letting go of their old behavior patterns and their relentless arguing for their limitations. They are encouraged by the *imemine* and their uncon-scious shadow behavior to which they are still emotionally addicted. They are frightened because they don't know how to break free or just aren't ready to let go, be loved, and blessed.

I encourage each of us to love ourselves anyway and to not resist the resistance of change. Transitioning from scarcity to prosperity, moving from lack to love, is a blessed journey not to be taken for granted because the withdrawal discomfort provides great insights and value. I encourage each of us to sincerely decide what we truly want and embrace our defi-ance to change so we may maximize what we learn from the resistance we encounter as we begin to lift the spell guarded by the *imemine* and enter the light. I encourage each of us to first define what we want, to be responsible, purposeful and committed, and then to commence the new journey of prosperity.

All that you devote your awareness to grows and thrives. How you choose to invest your energy is always in your hands: It is always your responsibility. Being human and having free will is in itself life's greatest blessing. By choosing to bless, you are choosing to live from the heart, not from your head.

The opportunity to be fully alive is always there in every moment. All that's required is to seize the moment and express gratitude.

Practicing Gratitude Toward Our Bodies

As soon as we make the choice to be grateful, appreciate our bodies, and treat them with love and respect, they spontaneously transform from being stressed out and tight to being calm and relaxed. They move from rejection to love. The pent-up tension diminishes, our breathing becomes deeper and freer, and our hearts have full rein to pulse. In our daily nour-ishing rituals, there are many opportunities to practice gratitude toward our body—the vehicle of our soul and the greatest measure of our spiritual well-being.

Most of us look at our bodies and say, "I don't want you. Not as you are." All that you ingest becomes your body, and your body is the temple of your soul. Both the nourishment that you choose and the attitude you have toward food reflect how you appear at the moment at which you ingest energy. Whether you are nourishing bitterness, anger, anxiety, or love, what you choose to nourish at any given moment is crucial.

When I speak to people about diet, I often joke that it could be extremely dangerous to eat healthy food because it means nourishing the *imemine* on high-energy sustenance. If you are harboring anger and bitterness, then that is what you are nourishing with whatever you ingest. The essential thing is to understand that food is energy, which is love, and if we feel gratitude and love for what we ingest, then the consequences will be quite different from feeling full of rejection or abandonment.

We have the opportunity many times every day to practice loving ourselves whenever we ingest anything and thereby to systematically eliminate the effects of unconscious rejection. The best way to do this is to decrease our intake of "unnatural" food (heavily processed and full of additives). When we do, a miracle awaits us. It means we have chosen to affirm that all nourishment is a declaration of love for our body: "If it passes my lips, it's love."

If you show your body trust and love, you will no longer experience resistance or rejection. By being aware and grateful for your blessings (both "good" and "bad"), you become prosperous, and that is how your strength and integrity increase. That is how you will experience prosperity—in the bliss of the moment.

A Dancer Who Resented Her Legs

One of the clearest examples I have seen of the power of love and gratitude is when a charming, lovely, and statuesque woman came to see me. She was a dancer, and in great physical shape, but she was tormented with resentment and anxiety.

Through spurts of crying she told me how she thought she was doing everything right as far as diet and physical training were concerned—but neither of them was having the desired effect on what she wanted to change: her legs. She wanted her legs to be different. She hated them, said they were stiff and deformed by thick cellulitis, and not in proportion with the rest of her body.

She was right. Her legs were not in proportion with her body, but they were strong, and in every other respect, beautiful legs that any woman would be glad to have.

She asked whether I could help her, and I immediately said that I could. "No question about it," I told her. "It's not difficult to transform this situation."

The emotional charge she had put into her dissatisfaction with her legs was awesome. It was pure hatred. I managed to persuade her that the only way to change her legs was to change her perspective—by moving from hatred to love, from cursing her legs to blessing them. My suggestion was that she engage in a love affair with her legs, fully appreciating them with all her heart for being part of her life and that she thank them for carrying her through life and for never letting her down.

I gave her the task of caring for her legs with love and attention at every opportunity, morning and night, when she dressed and undressed. She was to show her legs special care and attention in the bath by using an exfoliating glove and essential minerals.

Six months later, her legs were completely transformed. Now they were in proportion with the rest of her body. They were more flexible and the cellulitis had almost completely disappeared. Now, she was proud of her legs and her relationship with them and her foundation—the legs she had passionately resented for years. She bore herself quite differently after that, proud of her new standing. Most important, she now understood the power of love and gratitude.

A Grateful Heart Is a Generous One

Generosity is the ultimate human state. Generosity is unlimited gratitude. It is gratitude that is so abundant that it gives and gives because it is inexhaustible. It knows no shortage. It is light; it is life itself. When we are generous, we completely trust ourselves and have reinstated our power, our glow. Generosity is gratitude that has connected to the source, a free heart—a heart that is fully expressing itself.

Generosity reminds us that it is always *us*—us, me, you, him, her, all that is visible and all that is invisible. It is all the same energy. That is why it only requires one person to change the world, one person who chooses to love and stop rejecting. That person will change the energy in every cell of her body. She will change her message to the universe. This will have a chain reaction throughout the world and an effect on all who come into contact with her. It just takes one person to change the world, one person who brings about a miracle by changing perspectives, one person who *is* the change.

Liberation from Illusions

At this stage, we liberate ourselves from the illusions of the mind, the idea that we are thoughts and attitudes and not energy and love. That is why I encourage people to look inside themselves and see what matters most to them moment by moment—what matters at every single turning point they face. Either we continue as we have always done—drawn by the *imemine*—or we reach into our hearts and ignite a flame of passion there.

From time immemorial, spiritual beings have emphasized living the moment, not in the perceived past or the potential future. We can practice being in the present by conducting a little ceremony, such as lighting a candle and by being fully present in its glow. Being present means being completely empowered and able to devote the energy of love with pure intent and purpose. The image in my mind that best describes the intensity of the power of presence is recalling a time from my childhood when I used to play with a magnifying glass. I would use this glass to burn my initials or an image on to a piece of wood or to light fires by directing the rays of the sun through the magnifying glass. By collecting and concentrating the sun's energy through the glass, I was able to incinerate almost anything. By the same token, some people may need to reignite their own dying flame and retrieve themselves from their scarcity-based and fragmented thinking patterns. I always give thanks when I light or extinguish a candle because it brings me into the present moment and reminds me of the light in my life and the gratitude I feel for all that matters most to me in my life.

When present, I am collected and accountable; my energy, my light, my sunshine is at my command. Being present means being generous, unlimited, and unconstrained. "Generosity" means gratitude in action. The only way to insure and sustain prosperity is to share, to give, and to be generous. The attitude of gratitude is reflected by giving and trusting that the energy we devote always has positive nurturing effects and that by giving without attachment the energy will always find its way back to the giver. The old adage "We get what we give, and we give what we get" is still as sound as ever. Generosity is never limited or attached. It is boundless.

We connect to our friends and family through gifts, but it is not the intrinsic value of those gifts that matters but the feelings in our hearts when we give. It is our attitude that matters, what lies behind the gift, and often gratitude is the best gift of all.

Holding My Imemine at Bay with Gratitude

My *imemine* is very powerful, and I am so well acquainted with it that I ensure its passivity. Sometimes I require a particularly strong boundary around my prosperity to sustain the light and hold the *imemine* at bay. When I lapse into self-pity, a fully automatic-complaint mode seems to take over, one that detects faults in just about everything. I become sarcastic because sarcasm is the way a coward complains; he finds the weak spots in people and exploits those weaknesses. Of course, all this is done to disguise my own self-pity, my own idea that I am lacking in this or that respect—or that the wife has or hasn't done something, or the children have or haven't done something, or that my colleagues are acting in a particular way because of something I did or didn't do, and so on and so forth.

The game is on. The *imemine* tastes blood and immediately rises to the occasion. I know from my own experience that as soon as it is given an extended leash, it smells power and snarls with delight. Fortunately, I remember gratitude at these moments. I remember that being grateful is a choice, a decision where I devote attention consciously. And the fact is that most of us could actually write a very, very long list of all the things we have to be grateful for—every single day. I have no reason to compose such a list. As far as I am concerned, the following will suffice: *"I am grateful for each breath. I am grateful for my well-being. I am grateful for my family and my friends."*

Celebrating the Day as It Begins

One of the greatest opportunities presented to us as we near the conclusion of this book is to choose a lifestyle of prosperity. One suggestion is to exercise gratitude and review all the blessings we have attracted from the sincerity of our hearts; to lay ourselves to rest at night with the intention and the will to metabolize and assimilate these experiences as we sleep; to allow ourselves to count the blessings of the passing day and to become a part of the approaching light; and to renew in the present moment and prepare ourselves for the obvious blessings presented to us when we rise.

The ability to open our eyes in the morning and feel the air in our lungs and the blood flowing in our veins and to be able to shout out our thanks for being alive and dance and celebrate as we lie there in our beds. Not only is this opportunity present when we wake in the morning, but every time we remember ourselves in the moment.

The Act of Generosity

What matters most in this life is our immediate environment, our friends, and our family. When they die, we often begin to understand for the first time what they meant to us and what they contributed to our lives. Each time someone close to me passes, I perform a ceremony where I bless the passing being for what he or she contributed to my life. I thank that being from the depth of my heart for reminding me of how precious each moment of our lives is and for reminding me to live fully. We do not need to wait until their lives expire to express our gratitude.

When we awaken to prosperity consciousness, we are filled with gratitude. We are sincere. We live to be loving, caring, kind, and compassionate in every waking moment. We constantly express our generosity to those closest to us and to those not so close to us—whether they be family, friends, or colleagues. We do this actively, from the heart, by directing our awareness toward them without any attachment or agenda—just love.

When we live prosperity, gratitude pulsates in every cell of our being. To be able to give from generosity and gratitude is the greatest gift we have been presented with and therefore the greatest gift we can share. We live to give continuously, without attachments or conditions; we live to cultivate flowers and herbs that grow in our gardens and devote our full attention so that they thrive and grow. We live to understand and to feel that our existence is only cause and effect. We acknowledge that we are constantly attracting life to ourselves in resonance with the frequency of the heart—and this is why it is imperative that the heart be tuned to the fullest capacity of love and prosperity for expression. To be able to give fully and receive fully, the heart requires complete freedom.

The heart wants light.

The heart is light.

All else is illusion.

Gratitude Is Enlightenment

Our whole existence resides in the miniscule yet vast present moment that is, always. The moment is now and will always be now. Everything in the universe is as it should be. Gratitude is absolute proof that God is in me and in you and in all things.

> "To see a world in a grain of sand
> and a heaven in a wild flower,
> hold infinity in the palm of your hand
> and eternity in an hour."
>
> —William Blake

Yours is the power and always has been. We have misunderstood life, misunderstood the balance between the mind and the heart, and misunderstood the energy that is omnipresent. Yours is the power—all that is required is to be fully present, to choose to inhabit the present moment because will is power and might is bestowed on those who choose to be present.

Choose to be fully present in the full radiance of your soul. Attachment, incentives, carrots, and bonuses—they are all redundant. It is sufficient that you open your arms to receiving and your heart to giving. The embrace alone is adequate—what else is an embrace other than two hearts that choose to join? There are only opportunities in this life, and no problems—only the suffering that stems from rejection and resistance, and we have the power to step outside the vicious cycle of emotional constraints and personal abandonment. There is only light. Let us be the light.

In gratitude you are expressing your heart. The *imemine* does not understand gratitude, but gratitude is the only thing the heart understands. Gratitude is illumination. Illumination is gratitude. The only affirmation or prayer you will ever require is short, to the point, and always appropriate: "Thank you, sincerely."

Gratitude in Action

1. Count your blessings; create a ritual by blessings things that get your attention. Say thank you each time you awaken, literally, in the morning, and each time you become conscious of your environment.
2. Light candles and savor the light. Allow the light to infuse the light in your heart. When you extinguish the light, thank the light for its service.
3. Bless your water and food; bless every morsel of food you ingest. Thank Mother Earth for all she provides and be respectful of the energy you ingest and what you are intentionally and purposefully nourishing. Bless every sip of water that enters your lips and acknowledge that it is the essence of life on this planet.
4. Bless and create your day; each morning give thanks for being alive as you consciously envision how you want your day to progress and advance. Reaffirm your prosperity by reciting your favorite affirmation—for instance, "I command prosperity."

Conclusion

Thank you for reading this book for all of us. I know it contains a series of challenging perspectives, but I also trust at the same time I have reminded you of your inherent wisdom and divinity. I have not told you anything your heart does not already know. My intention has been to remind you of the wisdom that resides in your heart and of everything you are, always have been, and always will be. It has been to remind you that you are the creator and that your perspectives determine the outcome of your life.

The purpose of this book is to encourage you to awaken to the awesome power of the present moment and the might you have access to when you forgive yourself and become a responsible conscious creator. Always remember:

All that you devote your awareness to grows and thrives.

Purpose is the foundation of prosperity, and our purpose is always the same: to be love. How we express that purpose and how we choose to contribute is our responsibility. The nature of being is the nature of belonging. Resonating in harmony with all other hearts is the desire. The yearning that resounds in all our hearts continues until we connect with our heart and all other hearts in the same instance. Prosperity is our birthright and by transitioning from the duality of mind to the unity and sincerity of heart, our permission to be love is actualized and unfolds as we allow advancement. We therefore permit our liberated hearts to communicate our commitment by encouraging others to prosper, and by being and leading by example as we implement our will by acting consciously from insight with generosity and love.

When you believe in light, you will understand me when I say: God is light, and energy is light, and the heart is light, and love is light . . . love is all that matters.

daily reflections

Ask yourself the following questions and be prepared to record the answers in your notebook or journal. (Your response can be as simple as yes or no. If no, also answer why not. If yes, answer what that means and looks like to you.)

• Am I counting my blessings?

• Do I affirm gratitude?

• Am I complete—fully present and accounted for?

• What miracle am I intending today?

• Am I prosperous? Generous?

Appendix A

Personal Experiences with the Program

These following stories from a few clients who have taken my workshops or attended coaching sessions illustrate the changes that are possible when we follow the steps to prosperity. They show what happens when we become responsible for our lives and change our perspectives and dialogue from scarcity-based thinking and acting to prosperity consciousness.

A Change of Diet

I have always had food on my mind. My eating patterns have always been overindulgent. What I eat is too sweet and too fatty and I eat too often, too late at night, and sometimes in the middle of the night, too. Since I became an adult and responsible for myself, I have struggled inwardly and outwardly over what I put in my mouth because I have long known that my eating patterns are not exactly healthy. There have been occasional fumbling endeavors to control my consumption of food: diet planning, slimming, keeping a watch on my weight, exercise. But all the successes I have had are short-lived and limited, and in the end, always result in a denial that sounds something like this: "I am a loser who cannot control what I eat."

If someone had told me that I could, in seven weeks, alter my diet substantially for the better and *without having to struggle* I would simply have laughed at him. But that is exactly what happened when I attended Gudni's workshop.

I changed from being a typical unconscious eater to someone who could exclude white sugar, bleached flour, yeast, all dairy products, all additives (that is, as found in processed or fast food), pork, and chicken

In addition—and I actually thought this was impossible—for several weeks I stopped eating after six o'clock in the evening!

It is worth mentioning here that this took places in stages. For the first couple of weeks, we were allowed to eat fish and lamb; in the third week, fish and lamb were excluded and we were encouraged not to eat after six o'clock at night. We were also encouraged to slow down when we ate, to chew properly, and to nourish with full awareness. This led to automatically eating smaller portions because when we eat slowly we are present and recognize when we are satisfied.

I experienced a dramatic change in the way I felt physically on only the second day and that made it easier for me to strengthen my resolve—I wanted to sustain this feeling of well-being. I had more energy and the fluctuations in my energy levels disappeared—those fluctuations that had always meant that I had to eat something right now. What happened as a result was logical: I ate less without experiencing any loss of energy.

The greatest difference—and the one that I like the most—is that I only eat before six o'clock in the evening. Practicing this made it very clear that my understanding of hunger was skewed. I fully understood that previously I had consumed food for emotional purposes and to ward off my restlessness, irritability, boredom, and fear. I, who always thought I needed to eat large meals around eight o'clock at night and even to have some cookies or snack afterward, realized by eating at regular intervals during the day without consuming any additives or other high-sugar substances, I did not need to eat before going to bed. The nourishment I had during the day was sufficient to last until the following morning.

Now I eat 40 percent less food than before. At the same time, I am never hungry. Of course, I have lost some weight—which is not a bad thing since I was considerably more padded than I wanted to be—but dieting was not the aim or the goal. I want to continue this behavior because I feel much better, physically and psychologically.

I am no longer addicted to food. And that is a small miracle in itself, as far as I am concerned. I now understand what I lacked was a framework that included responsibility, purpose, and commitment—a caring discipline that follows a higher purpose more than simply dieting or improved physical appearance. It also helped to be part of a group as far as eating habits were concerned because we all encouraged and supported each other.

Perhaps the most difficult part about changing my eating pattern was dealing with other people's reactions—many people called me a self-depriving fanatic and belittled my achievements. What kept me going was precisely my commitment—I wanted to do it; I was ready to be responsible for my own consumption and my own physical condition. I had a tangible and meaningful purpose. The decision came from me, of my own free will, and I knew exactly why I was making the choice I wanted to be free of my addiction to absence.

Taking Responsibility

Alcohol played a large role in my life for twenty years. I had persuaded myself that I only drank to enjoy myself with my friends and that I had enough self-control to keep drinking in moderation. Although that's not how things turned out, I continued anyway, knowing deep down that if I wanted my life to flourish I had to stop.

Innumerable weekends came and went with all the usual things that go with drinking: throwing up, getting depressed, overeating, self-pity, list-lessness, and inertia. I tried time and again to stop but could never admit to myself or anyone else that I had a problem. The rejection that went along with all this was enormous and produced feelings of inadequacy and inferiority that impacted my daily life. I was convinced that I was doomed to perpetuate this pattern and there was nothing I could do to change it.

After attending three weeks of Gudni's workshop, I was finally able to face the fact that I was responsible for my drinking and all that the prob-lems that drinking caused or entailed. What was worse was that I was also responsible for how my future would turn out and all the consequences I could expect if I continued to drink. I was responsible for those days devoted to being hung over and disempowered. I was responsible for the disem-powerment that I brought on by rejecting myself. I finally understood that I was not a leaf in the wind, being pushed from one drink to another, and that the fact I was intoxicated was not because of my friends or because of my upbringing or because I was genetically predisposed to alcoholism.

I was entirely responsible.

That was quite a thing to admit to myself and I found myself getting angry inside when Gudni talked about being responsible on the first evening of the workshop. I was in serious denial as far as the idea of responsibil-ity was concerned. I had told myself for a long time that I wanted to stop drinking. On this evening of the workshop I understood that I did not want a change; I was frightened of change. Gudni helped me understand that I needed to admit it to myself and to my community and give myself the permission to enjoy what a life without alcohol had to offer. I took a look at how my drinking might affect my future and saw how it could prevent me from achieving my goals and have seriously adverse effects, to say the least, on what I intended as my purpose in life.

The thought of not drinking had first occurred to me many years ago, but this was the first time that I was ready to sit down at a table with twenty or so people and say no to a glass of wine and not be ashamed to explain why. I was ready to be true to myself, regardless of what anyone else might think. I felt an inner freedom and a great surcharge of energy. All of a sudden, I could run distances that I had convinced myself were impossible for me to manage. I had re-empowered myself, taken responsibility, and given myself permission to be true and to enjoy life.

Self-Care Responsibility

I often can't be bothered to take a shower and through the years I have used the following justifications for refraining: "I sleep badly if my hair is wet." "I need to wake up too early—and I'm not losing 30 minutes of sleep just to take a shower." "It's so good to curl up on the sofa when I get home."

And this kind of nonsense is endless—the mind struggles to find the right assertions and justifications each day in order to avoid taking a shower. I have probably had this inner conversation with myself ten thousand times. At the end of the day, the matter really is very simple: according to me I don't deserve to be clean and tidy. I don't deserve to look good because I "decided" many years ago that I wasn't one of those girls who bothered about her appearance. The truth was that I just didn't think I was good-looking enough to think about my appearance, and I used the opportunity to belittle those girls who did. "I can't be bothered . . . this is how I am . . . I'm different, and I'm not sufficiently x or I'm too y . . . " And you know what? Of course these reasons that ran through my head all the time convinced me I was right. We devote all our energy to conducting ourselves in accordance with such convictions and make sure they never go outside the framework we have created for ourselves. It is challenging to tell the truth about our assertions, and even though I have turned this stone over, there is an old assertion hiding somewhere, waiting for me to believe once again than I do not deserve to be neat, clean, and tidy.

That means that every day I have to be "shower responsible" and choose prosperity—to choose to shower and not listen to the old and tired whining of the *imemine* that does not want me to feel physically good and enjoy myself.

Demonizing People

I know a man who is very talented and a good guy in all respects. He is ambitious and pretty much knows what he wants in life. But he is stuck in a pattern of behavior that he has admitted to be noticeably holding him back and causes him to suffer:

"I am always demonizing people. It always happens when I take something on, both at work and socially. I always place myself in a subservient position with regard to whoever is in charge. This is normal enough in itself because I, of course, believe they bear greater responsibility than me on the final outcome. Usually, I am working for someone else in some capacity.

"But it is not fear of the boss that causes me trouble. What I find difficult is when my relationship with whoever is in charge is direct and unadulterated—when I feel I am doing what I should and that he trusts me.

"That is why I have consistently procrastinated about various projects. By delaying the natural progress of the job in hand, I immediately create a situation that is full of tension. And that's how I come to fear the disappointment of whoever is in charge.

"Sometimes, this is on a minor scale and sometimes I have done this with very large projects where a great deal was at stake, both financially and otherwise. It's a kind of poker game I play with energy, time, and my relationships with other people.

"The truth is, of course, that 'the boss' often reacts harshly and that is no surprise: I am cheating on what I am supposed to be doing. Fortunately, I've noticed this game I play. It is my way to confirm two ideas that are part of my story:

1) People cannot be trusted—and that they will always reprimand me in the end. And 2) I am not to be trusted—I will always let people down."

By acknowledging his patterns of self-sabotaging behavior and his motives for acting in this manner, this client was able to be aware and responsible for the energetic manipulation he was accustomed to, and then completely changed his relationships with his co-collaborators and reinstated his empowerment.

A Weekend in No-Man's-Land

I repeat the same behavior pattern every weekend. I work freelance and can decide how much time I devote to individual projects and how I organize them. When Friday comes around, I rarely let go and enjoy myself. Instead, I proceed directly into a vicious cycle of guilt. It goes something like this:

Some weekends I take the kids to the movies, out for a bite to eat, or to the zoo, or I just hang out at home on my own. I usually manage to enjoy this at first, but as soon as Saturday night arrives, a kind of tension sets in and begins to mount. On Sunday morning, the tension has reached a new peak, and I am both stressed and grouchy. This has a negative effect on the day. Sometimes things are so bad that I become very ill-tempered and intolerant with the kids, and Sundays often end with me distressed and the children unhappy.

Why does this happen? Because while I am "enjoying life" with the children, I can't escape the fact that I should be working. In the back of my mind, my obsessive thinking keeps nagging me, sounding something like this: *You shouldn't be at the zoo. You should be at work. You have plenty to do and have overrun a number of deadlines. What's more, you're broke. Why don't you let the kids watch some cartoons and just do some work? You don't deserve to be relaxing like this. You should be working.*

This is a strange way to live your life. It means living in a neither/nor situation—I can't enjoy my time with the kids, and I'm unable to work. I'm nowhere. The other side of the coin is when I do decide to work on the weekend instead of being with the kids, the nagging just gets turned around: *You shouldn't be working. You should be with the kids instead of having someone babysit them. Aren't they what's most precious in your life? What kind of a father works all weekend instead being with his children?*

I am nowhere—neither fully at work nor fully there for my kids. The punishment is twofold—self-deprecation and rejection. I am in no-man's-land—in a constant state of absence.

By acknowledging his absence and inability to be present, my client was able to see how his patterns were fueling one another and that it was his guilt and discomfort he was avoiding, not his children or his work. The moment he became responsible for this behavior, he was able to be aware of the emotions evoked by reacting unconsciously and chose to be present and aware, thereby diffusing the emotional charge triggered by these patterns and eventually rendering them completely passive.

He now enjoys being with his children, and obviously his children appreciate his presence. He also enjoys his work and is therefore much more productive, which benefits all.

The Big To-Do List

When the pressure of daily life became too great, I would make a long list of all the tasks I should be doing or needed to complete—what we usually call a to-do list, or itinerary. I felt relieved as soon as I had drawn up the list because there is substantial satisfaction to be derived from taking an initial action.

The next step would be to prioritize the items on the list. Some of them were minor (purchasing lightbulbs), while others were more complex and slightly daunting (filling out tax forms), and others greater in scope and more time-consuming (writing a book).

The following morning, I would look at the list and select a few tasks to carry out. Sometimes, I chose one large task and three small ones. Sometimes, I postponed one of the more challenging tasks and eagerly finished off several small ones instead. By evening, I could honestly feel that I had a very productive day.

The next day, the whole game would begin again—a game I call "making headway." Sometimes, I did very well two or three days at a time. But in the end, I always abandoned the plan. Never consciously. I never threw the list away. It always disappeared without my noticing it. After two to three days of carrying out tasks, I would stop referring to the list in the mornings, and it would remain in the back pocket of my pants or somewhere it was ultimately forgotten.

That was fine in itself, I suppose. But this lip service to discipline simply empowered the *imemine*. When I abandoned my intentions, two new voices would join my inner choir:

One says, *The chores are still there, mounting up . . .*

And the other one says, *Honestly, you can't even keep to your commitments when they are written and staring you in the face!*

The plan ("making headway") that was supposed to liberate me and make my life easier backfired, and I used it to criticize myself.

Today, I have a different view of list making. I realize that it has only limited use and that I have to be very careful about what items I place on it. The list is a framework for freedom that must not mutate into one about absence and self-criticism.

Creating lists and setting goals is always a great idea. People who create lists and set up goals are reported to achieve up to 50 percent more results than those who don't. Many weight-loss programs have substantiated that the participants who record their consumption reduce their body weight up to 50 percent faster than those who don't. So just by putting pen to paper, we are progressing and advancing. However, the whole idea here is to progress in conjunction with how worthy we feel, and this process cannot be cheated or forced. So whatever plans your making or to-do lists you write make sure you're not exceeding your worthiness allowance.

Now There's Only One Type of Food

As far as I was concerned, there were always two types of food: food that was good for me and food that I liked. When I ate food I knew was good for me, I felt good, and because I had grown up in a household where wholesome food was abundant I did not have many opportunities to use food to reject myself until I left home. As a child, I felt deprived because there were so many restrictions on my diet.

For ten years after leaving home, I ate only food that tasted good to me. But every time I ate a burger, a sandwich, bread, cheese, or meat, or drank soda pop, a little voice whispered inside me, *You know this is not good for you. Why are you eating such unwholesome food?* And as soon as it spoke, I rejected myself for consuming the very food I chose to eat of my own free will.

At the end of the ten years, I radically changed my diet for the better. My eating patterns were not serving my waistline or my energy levels, and I was becoming exceedingly negative and even aggressive toward myself for my unwholesome eating habits. But the rejection process continued. Whenever I strayed from the path, I experienced anger and used every ice-cream cone and burger to drag myself down into the mire. In my mind, I was always supposed to be on the straight and narrow—and I condemned any deviation.

After much hardship, I enrolled in Gudni's workshop "The Power of Awareness." Through the work, I gained insight and realized that freedom did not consist in resisting temptation, but in allowing myself to deviate from my rules every now and again without chastising myself. I saw and understood that the effects of guilt and rejection on my body were far greater than the effects I felt when I ate a burger, ice cream, or slice of chocolate cake. Now, there is only one type of food—all the food I eat and therefore all the food I love.

Appendix B

A Note About the 12 Steps

I have many good friends who have transformed themselves according to the 12 Steps of Alcoholics Anonymous (AA). They are good examples of a system that can help people improve their lives. Sometimes, however, people have intimated that my ideas are contrary with those of the 12 Steps. I do not agree. The core of what I have to say can be basically reduced to two things: 1) by ridding ourselves of a damaging and persistent absence we regain our energy, and 2) that we find all the true strength that lies within us. Actually, the 12 steps do talk about believing in and trusting a higher power, but the nature of that higher power is left to the individual to determine or decide. And many people who adhere to the 12-step system see God as the best possible version of themselves, some kind of perfect truth, steadfastness, and freedom. This idea is in perfect harmony with my ideas: we are the power and the glory and that is our responsibility.

Even though one speaks of a higher power in the 12-step program, the fact is all the progress is based on the initiative of the individual. The 12-steps are not something one goes through to be healed. You do the healing by going through each stage and take the steps to be responsible for your life.

Our faith never exceeds beyond ourselves. If we don't believe in ourselves or our own power, we cannot believe in anything else, beyond our own faith. To truly connect with this energy, with nature, and with a higher power, we need to begin by connecting with ourselves and our personal source of light.

The wind

whether we can know
where the path lies

where to look
and when to look away

when to enter
and when to exit

when we may cry
and how

when to pause
and pick up stones

whether the wind sweeps us away

and never to know
where the path lies

to know whether
the wind sweeps us from the path

or

whether it is the path

—Davið Stefánsson

Glossary

"In the beginning there was the word." This powerful statement indicates that creation began with language and how and what we create is an expression of prosperity and love or an expression of scarcity and fear. Conscious language is a powerful tool and resource for being aware, sustaining presence, and being a deliberate creator. The immense power of the spoken word comes not only from the meaning of the word but also from the tone and vibration used when delivered. When we begin to listen to the words we use and how we use them, we enter into a new way of being. We awaken to the realization that language creates positive or negative energy. Dispense this energy with wisdom.

This glossary contains many of the terms that I have used throughout this book. While the words themselves may be familiar to you, the manner in which I have used some of them may be new to you. Familiarizing yourself with their meaning will help you along this journey toward prosperity and gratitude.

Absence (to be absent)—Distracted, fragmented, scattered, unconscious, absentminded, generally due to guilt, remorse, or regret. The opposite of presence and responsibility.

Addiction—Obsession, instinctive urges and appetites, automatic reactions based on emotional attachments.

Adult—To be fully responsible, in full blossom.

Anxiety—Ingratitude. A choice one makes by choosing to not let go and accept responsibility for one's life. It is a lack of trust and not being trustworthy; it is the anticipation of failure based on one's belief system. (When you trust yourself, you trust life, and there is no reason to be anxious.)

Attachments—Thought patterns, doubts, and criticisms used to constrain and condition our existence. Attachments are always based on the assumptions we use to validate the way we live. We use them to market our perspectives, the story we have chosen to tell about our lives, and our hidden agendas.

Awareness—Love; energy; a light that shines unconditionally. The key to transformation. Awareness is your primary asset.

Being—To permit oneself to be; as in human *being*, not human *doing*.

Believe—To trust and strengthen oneself.

Boring (to be bored)—A perspective of resistance or defiance.

Cause and effect—The rule of the universe.

Charge—Energy devoted or invested in something; when there is a great deal of emotional charge, we are investing a great deal of energy to sustain it.

Collective unconscious—According to Carl Jung, this is the archetypal, universal mental predispositions that are not necessarily grounded in our personal experiences. I sometimes refer to the collective unconscious as the spiritual Internet, which we are accessing and downloading information from in the form of thought forms or ideas floating around in the ether or field of infinite possibilities.

Commitment—To give oneself completely and clearly announce to the world what is truly desired.

Conquer/Dominate—Arrogant exhibitionism; overkill.

Conscience—Mutual awareness, collective wisdom; the knowledge of the heart, which is accessible to everyone.

Constraint or suffering—The inability to express or share oneself.

Courageous—To be of the core, or heart, to have the energy to show up fully.

Decide—To become empowered; the conscious choice of intending one's own life.

Dis-ease—To be absent, out of balance, not at ease, fragmented, not whole. There is only one dis-ease: a constrained heart.

Disappointment—Not showing up for oneself; not doing what it takes to create the desired outcome; deploying hope or disillusion instead of action.

Ego—*See* **Imemine**.

Emotion—Something moved or stirred; all emotion is a sense of feeling, and all feeling is a sense of being.

Emotional bankruptcy—Exhausted and depleted by investing and devoting the energy to self-betrayal and abandonment.

Empowerment—The power to choose one's own mode of existence— what one does in life and how he or she chooses to act.

Energy—All there is; everything. It is a current that cannot be extinguished. There are various expressions of energy. Some frequencies are long, others short. But all life is energy—all that is lives in motion, waves, and frequencies. One's energy is his or hers to invest however one chooses. It can be invested in feeling good or bad just as it can be used to nourish the *imemine* or the heart.

Excuses—Thoughts or judgments we use to weigh down our existence to justify not taking action. The only reason to argue for a limitation is to limit our prosperity and to sustain how we truly feel about ourselves. Excuses are a powerful tool to sustain the spell of the *imemine*. They are always based on "principles" that justify our limited existence. An excuse is also the marketing of our attitudes and point of view to reinforce ideas and the version of our life we have chosen to tell and live by.

Feeling bad—Depressed, weighed down, restrained movement, restrained motion, being absent.

Forgive—To purge, to relieve ourselves, let go, lighten our load, and unclench our fists.

Freedom—Complete responsibility; to judge nothing and no one.

Generosity—To give in complete faith and in true prosperity. Generosity breeds abundance.

Gorging/bingeing—Nourishing absence, distance, misery, and lack.

Greed—Lack of love, an open wound of emptiness that will not heal.

Heart—The unified field of integrity. The heart is the Emperor; when we live and create from the unity of the heart, we are aligned with the universe, in harmony with all creation, and all that we manifest is permission based and whole. Heart equals generosity, trust, abundance, and prosperity.

Honesty—A commitment to keep our word.

Hope—A reflection of shame or guilt; a statement of arrogance and absence.

Hopeless—Free of illusions.

Human being—An energy transformer.

Imemine—The subconscious part of us, which some refer to as the ego, inner child, or shadow. It is opinion, judgment, criticism, praise, superiority, pride, and so on. The *i-me-mine* comprises all of the views and opinions we take personally. The *imemine* represents the appearance of selfhood that is greedy, selfish, and delusional. This part of us is reactive and impulsive, and its irrational behavior is based on programming from the collective unconscious. It is not who we are, although we sustain its illusionary existence and dominance for as long as we subscribe to victimhood and powerlessness.

The *imemine* is a lack of light; it is governed by ingratitude. It can also be seen as a parasite that thrives on deficiency and pretends to measure whether we are more or less than the people around us. It always operates from the duality of the mind and not from the integrity of the heart. Whoever lives according to the laws dictated by the *imemine* inhabits a very restricted dimension of existence—he or she is merely a talking head. The *imemine* is always in a position of lack. It lives like any other creature of instinct. It can always find something about us that does not measure up or can't measure down. The *imemine* thrives entirely on illusion. Indeed, it is illusion, and its only function is to maintain a high degree of separation and doubt. Embrace unity, and the *imemine* disappears until it is summoned again. The moment you're present and unified, the illusion of duality evaporates. Now there is only light, love, no shadow, doubt.

Impatience—Not having the endurance to be present.

Intention—Stretching out, saddling the horse, getting ready to set out on a journey. It is very easy to confuse intention with actually accomplishing a task or taking any direct action.

Intimacy—The ability to allow yourself and others to see you as you are. Being present.

Irritation—Trembling defiance; not taking responsibility for feeling sorry for yourself.

Lack and scarcity—The illusion fostered by the marketing systems we have co-created and sustain with our feelings of inadequacy and not being present; they are intended to fuel the economy, consciously or unconsciously. (Create the illusion of need and then provide the solution.) We have become distraction addicts who are in a perpetual state of loss and deprivation.

Light—Love, the origin of life. In the beginning, there was light.

Love—Light, the illuminated heart. The only emotion. All else is illusion.

Mind—An image processor and projector; a highly evolved computer that is either motivated by fear, lack, interest, or curiosity or inspired by awareness and purposeful vision and passion. The mind is like an amphitheater. (What is the story you're projecting onto the field of infinite possibilities?)

Miracle—A change of perspective; an action full of power; an action based on purpose, vision, and goals.

Mistake—An activity or invested energy that we have chosen to deem as negative; a way to punish ourselves. Mistakes are illusory.

Nourish—To be present and consciously ingest energy, love, and light. To nourish means to intentionally invest the energy of the mother to sustain prosperity and love. (You can feed lack, but you nourish love.)

Obsession—No differentiation between mind and consciousness; we think we *are* our thoughts.

Opportunity—Any disturbance encountered. Problems become challenges, which become opportunities.

Out of this world—Completely absent.

Pain—Exhaustion.

Patience—The ability to tolerate waiting for something and endure and therefore be abused. Patience is not a virtue; it is oppression. When present, there is no need for patience because there is no resistance to being in the moment. It is the difference between *being* in line and *waiting* in line.

Pattern/Habit—A chosen method of behavior we create through repetitive reactions to something. Habits are promoted out of absence. Unconscious, impulsive reactions are that of an animal where one's response is not being consciously chosen. To be a creature of habit means to be addicted, powerless, and incapacitated; it means the *imemine* is in charge.

Permission—The scale or degree of how much prosperity allowance we have determined.

Power—Free will/choice asserted through conscious devotion; presence. To be empowered by the knowledge that you have free will and are fully responsible for you own life, breath by breath. We often associate the word *power* with violence and oppression of the strong against the weak—"overpowering," "the powers that be," "the power to enforce," and so on. This use of the word is valid enough. However, in this book the word *power* has a different meaning.

Prana—The energy or electricity that we have at our disposal at any given time.

Problem—An illusion. An opportunity to divest or devote energy.

Procrastination—A decision to reject and diminish oneself in the now and therefore limit and constrain future possibilities. Procrastination is the most powerful way to betray oneself and suppress life force and energy. Procrastination is personal betrayal and a clear message or statement to the subconscious that we do not feel worthy of what we say we want. Each betrayal is subtle; however, they add up and eventually become poisonous and even lethal. Each time we procrastinate, we abandon ourselves and reject love and prosperity.

Prosperity—To thrive and be in a perpetual state of abundance: a life of holistic well-being and all-around affluence. A constant state of gratitude and trust-worthiness expressed with generosity; living fully from the heart. All is energy, energy is light, light is awareness, awareness is love, love is well-being, well-being is prosperity, and prosperity is living in abundance and generosity, trusting that there will always be enough.

Reality—Entertaining illusion; self-inflicted pain. Reality means having substance (that which is tangible), but it is perceived and therefore varies from individual to individual.

Rejection—Any resistance against the present moment, against oneself, against other people, or against situations in one's life. It is all the lack that can be imagined. Rejection means not wanting to be as you are now or not wanting others or things to be as they are now. Although rejection itself is never personal, the experience of rejection is always personal. Rejection is living according to the creed that the glass is either half empty or half full when, in fact, the glass is always full to the brim. Rejection is always a denial of love and prosperity.

Release—To let oneself be in the present moment.

Remorse and regret—The residue of unprocessed guilt and past behavior that we have not become responsible for and have therefore not forgiven ourselves. These are stories from the so-called past that change depending on how we feel and what we feel we need to manipulate each time. We are constantly attempting to prove ourselves right, constantly managing our belief systems or perspectives, managing our permission for prosperity or lack.

Resistance/Defiance—The most common way to avoid or suppress the anxiety we feel as a consequence of our lifestyles. While it can be one of the most stress-producing phenomena in modern life, resistance is an opportunity to grow. Resistance to any given challenge tells its own story and reveals something about us. By looking at it in a positive manner, we can learn from it and grow.

Responsibility—The ability to respond. Being "response-able" is the opposite of an unconscious, impulsive reaction. We have been far too quick to associate the word "responsibility" with guilt and duty—that there is something wrong with us if we do not meet our social obligations. In the courses I teach and here in this book, I encourage people to *be* responsible for their own existence (not to *shoulder* or *bear* the responsibility), because being responsible is the key to prosperity. Without absolute responsibility there is no prosperity.

Sarcasm—the complaint of the coward; a way to try to influence the world without being responsible for change.

Scarcity consciousness—Absence and inability to be responsible for one's life; the refusal to be an adult. It is the perspective of victimhood, martyrdom, and deficiency. It is the argument of limitations.

Serious—Weighed down, grave, defensive.

Shame—The basis of guilt; we are always the source of our own shame.

Sincere—Operating solely from the heart; not from the duality of the head.

Stressed—Not wanting to be as we are, here and now, ungrateful.

Thoughts—Images projected by the mind. Our thoughts are pictures and the more vivid and clear they are, the faster they are manifested or materialized. We are not our thoughts although our thoughts become things. Our thoughts have no meaning or value unless we attach value or meaning to them; they just stream through the mind as bits of irrelevant information until we attach meaning to them. Thoughts aren't even personal until we make them personal and often times we don't even know where they came from.

Tired—Devoted to constraint and scarcity.

Trust—To strengthen ourselves and others.

Trustworthy—To be worthy of your own trust. It is not until you have proven yourself to be worthy and sustain your own discipline that you will trust yourself.

Twitch—An automatic or unconscious reaction; a pattern of behavior we do not want to reveal but from which we cannot escape; the unconscious behavior of the *imemine*.

un-, in-, im- —The most common prefixes in today's world; the most powerful and underhanded ways of abandoning oneself through language; for example: *un*believable, *im*possible, *in*coherent. All of these argue for limitations, not for scope. A display of absence.

Vulnerability—The ability to receive, to be accessible, trusting ourselves enough to deal with challenges or conflict. Vulnerability means to be present.

Waiting—Resisting the present; wanting things to be different.

Weak—Not being strong; to be diseased.

When-disease—A disease in which a person lives only in the future, never experiencing the *now*. Those who are afflicted with this disease are people who live their lives rejecting the present moment, who have developed a highly sophisticated means of sustaining absence, who persuade themselves they will be happy *when* . . . *when* I get married, *when* I have children, *when* I finish college. . . . Those who have the when-disease can never simply *be* in the present and can therefore never experience true prosperity.

Wholeness—To be whole, complete, present in the here and now.

Work—A task that has effective results, as in "it works."

Worth/Worthiness—The extent to which we allow ourselves (consciously or unconsciously) to experience love and prosperity. Knowingly or unknowingly, we keep an account of our past experiences; the way we have treated ourselves has left us either with a surplus or deficit of light and prosperity. Self-worth is how deserving we feel. When we decide to forgive and love ourselves and thereby feel worthy, it is then that we can accept the gifts of existence without incurring any disease. Worthiness is manifested in the prosperity we express and the light, energy, and love we are capable of receiving unconditionally.

Wound—Constant lack, the abyss of the soul.